IPS

The Counterforce Syndrome:

A Guide to U.S. Nuclear Weapons and Strategic Doctrine

Robert C. Aldridge

The Institute for Policy Studies is a nonpartisan research institute. The views expressed in this study are solely those of the author.

Published by the Institute for Policy Studies.

Copies of this book are available from the Institute for Policy Studies, 1901 Q Street, N.W., Washington, D.C. 20009 or The Transnational Institute, Paulus Potterstraat 20, 1071 DA, Amsterdam, Holland.

First Printing, 1978
Second Edition, 1979
Second Printing, 1981

Library of Congress Catalog Number 77-99156
ISBN 0-89758-008-7

About the Author

Robert Aldridge was born in Watsonville, California on April 15, 1926 where he grew up. During World War II he saw action with the 25th Division artillery in the Pacific and was in Manila when the Philippines received its independence on July 4, 1946.

After the war he studied aeronautical engineering; starting at California Polytechnic University in San Luis Obispo and then graduating magna cum laude from San Jose State University. He married Janet Balvin of South Dakota and they raised ten children.

Bob started work for Lockheed in 1957 when they built their missile plant at Sunnyvale, California. The first Polaris submarine-launched ballistic missile program was just beginning at that time and he subsequently helped design three generations of Polaris, the multiple individually-targeted reentry vehicles for Poseidon, and worked on the beginning of the Trident program.

When Trident design studies began in 1970, Bob was engineering group leader of an advanced design team in reentry systems engineering. He was assigned concept definition responsibility for the Mark-500 maneuvering warhead. In that capacity he first saw the shift to a more aggressive nuclear policy. In February, 1973 he resigned his engineering position in protest to the type of weapon that Trident was shaping up to be.

Since leaving Lockheed Bob has spent full time researching, writing, and lecturing on the nuclear arms race and the military-industrial complex. He has given special attention to the first-strike nature of weapons being developed. He and Janet also work with Pacific Life Community, a direct action oriented group experimenting with nonviolent methods of social change. They live in Santa Clara, California.

Contents

List of Figures

Preface to First Edition

Ten years ago I would not have written this pamphlet. Until recently I have not been a Pentagon critic. During my sixteen years in the engineering department of Lockheed, the nation's number one arms producer, I helped design every submarine-launched ballistic missile the Navy has bought. I was deeply entrenched in that work, and my future as an engineer was assured.

Many things led to my ultimate resignation from Lockheed, but seeing a nuclear policy shift had the most profound effect. At the onset of the Trident missile program, I discovered the Pentagon's interest in acquiring a precise "counterforce" weapon capable of destroying "hardened" military emplacements such as missile silos. This was a profound shift from a policy of retaliating only when fired upon, because it does not make sense to attack empty silos (which is all that would be left following an enemy first-strike on the United States).

Since leaving aerospace work I have spent full time research-ing, writing, and lecturing on the nuclear arms race. I have tried to use my experience and education to gather highly technical and widely isolated facts and present them in language under-standable to the layperson. My focus has been on the counter-force trend of emerging technologies which are leading the United States toward a preemptive first-strike posture. The masking of the evidence from public view is what I consider the grossest deception ever perpetrated on the American people.

It took a strong shock to pry me from that engineering career and financial security but the sinister behavior I witnessed was enough to create the needed jolt. My goal here is to pass along the substance of that jolt. Our main hope, as I see it, lies in an informed public interested in universal justice and motivated to make it happen. If this pamphlet provides some impetus toward that end I will feel well rewarded.

Robert C. Aldridge
Santa Clara, California
October 4, 1977

Preface to Second Edition

Many events have transpired since the first edition of this pamphlet was published. It has been read by many concerned people and, I hope, has increased public awareness of the evolving first-strike technologies. At least some people—not only Americans but also Japanese, Canadians, New Zealanders, and Australians—have told me they have been moved to action after reading it.

This booklet has also been reviewed by the Air Force as a publication which key Defense Department personnel should be aware in the official performance of their duties. In addition, the term "disarming first strike" is now frequently used both by Pentagon officials and by their critics. I would like to think this pamphlet has played a role in bringing about that debate.

In July 1978 this booklet was published in Tokyo in the Japanese language. During that month the first printing of 50,000 copies was sold out and it became number two on the nonfiction best seller list. I am encouraged that the people of Japan are so deeply concerned about America's military activities.

But publicity does not imply policy changes. The Pentagon's death technologies have taken significant strides and a disarming first-strike capability will start becoming reality by the mid-1980's unless corrective action is taken—unless the people of this country cease to accept the military's prescription for solving international disputes. If that first-strike capability materializes, we can expect nuclear weapons to be used in some way before the year 2000.

Time is short. All of these first-strike programs will be in or near production by 1982 or 1983. If the razor edge of the first-strike machinery is not dulled by that time it is unlikely that such a destabilizing capability could be stopped once the economic investment curve starts to rise steeply.

So the next three years are crucial—either we halt this momentum toward genocide or nuclear cremation will strike again. I have been criticized for sounding so pessimistic and dimming the hopes of those with long range plans, but my engineering interpretation tells me we have a near-term emergency on our hands. We will have to stop Trident and Missile-X immediately if we are to enjoy extended plans for changing public attitudes and priorities. I hope the second edition of *The Counterforce Syndrome* conveys the unmitigated urgency of this point.

Robert C. Aldridge
Santa Clara, California
July 15, 1979

Introduction

The purpose of this pamphlet is to provide between the covers of a single document a summary of U.S. strategic* nuclear weapons and military doctrine. One of the most difficult subjects to comprehend is military strategy. Highly technical in nature, it is further obscured by scientific jargon, security classifications, and fragmentation in many sources.

Nevertheless, military activities touch each of our lives intimately. It behooves us to have some understanding of what is taking place because we are the ones who pay for those weapons and will suffer from their misuse. Besides detracting from our own quality of life, America's arms programs also place the moral blame squarely on our shoulders for the suffering and oppression they cause in other lands. It is our personal action, or lack of action, that sustains the nuclear arms race and provides the weapons which inflame hostilities among smaller nations. We cannot afford to be uninformed.

This pamphlet is, of course, only a brief sketch, but it will cover the full range of Pentagon activity in the strategic area. Brevity is intentional for the sake of simplicity. Technical language is minimized but a glossary is provided for the terms used.

Deterrence

Deterrence is the strategic policy under which most of us believe the Pentagon is still operating. It is presented as a defensive measure, of sorts, because it is based on a second-strike response—massive and unacceptable retaliation—which theoretically deters the Soviet Union from attacking us. In order to be effective as a deterrent, U.S. retaliatory forces must be able to survive the worst conceivable enemy attack *and still* cause massive destruction in the Soviet Union. For this reason, America's land-based missiles are stored in underground silos which have been "hardened" (i.e., covered with massive concrete shields) to withstand an atomic blast, and a large portion of the strategic force has been placed on submarines which are relatively immune to detection and attack. These protective

---

*"Strategic" weapons are those weapons intended for use in an all-out thermonuclear war with the Soviet Union, such as intercontinental ballistic missiles (ICBMs), missile submarines, and heavy bombers.

measures are designed to provide the United States an "assured (second-strike) destruction" capability; when both superpowers have such a capability, as has been true since the late 1960s, we have the condition known as "mutual assured destruction," or, appropriately, MAD. Since MAD theoretically deters *both* sides from initiating a nuclear war, the United States and the Soviet Union agreed, in the 1972 Strategic Arms Limitations agreements (SALT-I), to refrain from deploying elaborate anti-missile defense systems (ABMs) and to freeze the number of offensive missiles possessed by each side.

Recent estimates indicate that as much as 24.8 percent of the Soviet population and 50 percent of the U.S.S.R.'s industry are concentrated in the top 100 Russian cities. That means, according to Defense Department parameters, 100 small bombs would inflict the necessary destruction to be a workable deterrent.

To effectively deter a Soviet attack on the United States, our strategic weapons should presumably be aimed at Russian cities and industrial areas. Those types of targets are vulnerable and our missiles would not have to be very powerful or particularly accurate. One 50-kiloton bomb, for instance, exploding within half a mile of a city's center, would incinerate the populace. What the much smaller 12½-20 kiloton bombs used at Hiroshima and Nagasaki did to those cities stands as evidence to that. (A kiloton is the nuclear explosive force equal to one thousand tons of conventional explosives. A megaton is equal to one million tons.)

What would the Soviets consider unacceptable retaliation and thus prevent them from launching a nuclear strike? In 1967, then Secretary of Defense Robert McNamara testified: "It seems reasonable to assume that in the case of the Soviet Union, the destruction of, say, one-fifth to one-fourth of its population and one-half to two-thirds of its industrial capacity would mean its elimination as a major power for many years."[1] Recent estimates indicate that as much as 24.8 percent of the Soviet population and 50 percent of the U.S.S.R.'s industry are concentrated in the top 100 Russian cities.[2] That means, according to Defense Department parameters, 100 small bombs would inflict the necessary destruction to be a workable deterrent. Allowing for repairs and maintenance, misfires, Soviet defenses, and a hypothetical Chinese threat, 400 warheads would constitute a more-than-adequate deterrence capability. Yet *more* than that number remain safely out of reach of Soviet attack in only *three* of America's 31 Poseidon missile submarines. Why then, we are justified in asking, have we such an overpowering overkill? The U.S. nuclear arsenal now contains over 30,000 nuclear bombs, some 22,000 so-called tactical nuclear weapons,* and approximately 10,000 strategic devices. Under the deterrent philosophy those numbers do not make sense. The very existence of so many weapons implies a darker and more sinister military doctrine.

More recently, apparently to justify the extreme silo-killing accuracy of forthcoming strategic missiles, the Defense Department has expanded the definition of deterrence by introducing the concept of counter-retaliation and counter-deterrence. Pentagon officials postulate an implausible scenario: suppose the Russians should launch an attack on U.S. missile silos but hold back a sizeable portion of their silo-based missile force to deter the United States from retaliating against Soviet cities by threatening counter-retaliation against American cities. In such a case, military experts claim, the U.S. must have weapons accurate enough to wipe out those silos at the same time it retaliates against Soviet urban-industrial targets.

Nevertheless, if American missiles can destroy Soviet silos in a second strike during the tensions of a nuclear war when response is expected and Soviet missiles are in a high state of readiness, then they can do it much more easily in a first strike when the opportune time can be picked and the element of surprise is in their favor. Destruction of silos is known as *counterforce* (a concept explained more thoroughly below). The destabilizing nature of counterforce is emphasized in a Congressional Budget Office background paper:

> *. . . There may be an inescapable dilemma in the procurement of second-strike counterforce capability: a U.S. arsenal large enough to attack Soviet ICBMs after having absorbed a Soviet first strike would be large enough to threaten the Soviet ICBM force in a U.S. first strike. Moreover, the Soviet Union, looking at capabilities rather than intentions, might see a U.S. second-strike capability in this light. Faced with a threat to*

---

*"Tactical" nuclear weapons are intended for battlefield use against enemy field forces—warships, tank formations, airfields, etc.—rather than, as in the case of *strategic* weapons, the enemy's urban-industrial heartland. Other than this difference in usage, there is no real difference between tactical and strategic nuclear weapons themselves, although of course the *delivery system* employed may vary.

their ICBM force, Soviet leaders facing an international crisis might have an incentive to use their missiles in a preemptive strike before they could be destroyed by the United States.[3]

It is not difficult to see the dangers of designing and deploying silo-killing missiles under the guise of deterrence. Besides providing a critical element in a first-strike scenario (as will be described later), they bring the prospect of nuclear war much closer—especially during times of international tensions, and those times are becoming more plentiful.

Counterforce

Counterforce has offensive connotations. By definition, it means that nuclear missiles are aimed at strategic military targets in the Soviet Union such as missile silos, nuclear stockpiles, and command and communications centers. Since these targets are "hard"—deeply entrenched and coated with thick concrete—a high explosive force is desirable and precision is mandatory. These are the targets of a disabling nuclear strike.

It appears that counterforce has been the Pentagon's clandestine military doctrine since at least the 1950s, even when the announced policy has been deterrence. Indeed, there has always been a schism between official, public policy and the operational doctrine that guides military planning. In a 1956 discussion of the word "policy," for instance, former Deputy Secretary of Defense Paul Nitze is quoted as saying, "In one sense, the action sense, it refers to the general guidelines which we believe should and will in fact govern our actions in various contingencies. In the other sense, the declaratory sense, it refers to policy statements which have as their sum political and psychological effects."[4] Almost 20 years later, Defense Secretary James Schlesinger confirmed that the "action" side of U.S. nuclear strategy has long incorporated a significant counterforce option when he wrote that: "several targeting options, including military only and military plus urban/industrial variations, have been part of U.S. strategic doctrine *for quite some time.*"[5] (Emphasis added.)

Robert McNamara provided what was probably the first official public admission of counterforce during a commencement address at the University of Michigan in Ann Arbor, on June 16, 1962. He stated that the United States' "principal military objectives in the event of a nuclear war stemming from a major attack on the alliance, should be the destruction of the enemy's military forces, not his civilian population."[6] That was the beginning, at least publicly, of the "damage limitation" theory

4

which became so popular in military circles. The ostensible aim was to limit damage to American cities in a nuclear war by destroying that portion of the Soviet missile force which may have been *held back* from a first strike. But, as shown above, damage limitation is at least as effective in a first-strike as in a second-strike response.

In 1967, the United States reached its peak deployment of 1,054 intercontinental ballistic missiles (ICBMs). In April of that same year the 41st and final Polaris missile-launching submarine was commissioned. McNamara declared that enough was enough—at least so far as *numbers* were concerned; henceforth the emphasis would be on *quality* rather than *quantity*. Although this focus on weapons sophistication made it more difficult to conceal the Pentagon's underlying counterforce intentions, two apparently valid reasons were given for the announced shift. First, given an obvious overkill capability so far as Soviet cities were concerned, it was becoming increasingly difficult to justify more and more missiles, and quality became easier to sell to Congress and the people. Second, the Soviets were also building ICBMs and missile launching submarines, and had started work on an anti-ballistic missile (ABM) system around Moscow, thus calling into question the "assured destruction" capacity of U.S. retaliatory forces. To counter that presumed threat, McNamara ordered the development of MIRVs, multiple independently-targeted re-entry vehicles, which could strike several targets simultaneously and thus overwhelm ABMs by sheer number of warheads.* As we shall see, however, the development of MIRVs also enhances the first-strike capabilities of U.S. forces.

McNamara initiated other qualitative improvement programs which have transformed the U.S. strategic arsenal. In 1966 he launched the Strategic Exercise Study (Strat-X) to consider alternate weapons configurations (mobile launchers, air-launched missiles, etc.), some of which will play a role in the Pentagon's new Missile-X (M-X) program. Work also began at this time on design studies for the proposed Underwater Long-range Missile System (ULMS), later known as Trident, and on an advanced manned strategic bomber, which later emerged as the B-1.

The Nixon Administration accelerated the drive for enhanced counterforce capabilities. In April 1969, only three months after Richard Nixon took office, Defense Secretary Melvin Laird requested funds "to significantly improve the accuracies of

---

*For a description of how MIRV works, see the section on "MIRVs and MARVs" below.

5

Poseidon missiles," thus signaling an offensive intent (since accuracy improvements were not needed for a retaliatory strike). This proposal was defeated in Congress at the time, but subsequently surfaced in other guises described later.[7] At about the same time, Nixon called for development of a limited counterforce capability on the grounds that:

Should the President, in the event of nuclear attack, be left with the single option of ordering the mass destruction of enemy civilians in the face of the certainty that it would be followed by the mass slaughter of Americans? Should the concept of assured destruction be narrowly defined and should it be the only measure of our ability to deter the variety of threats we might face?[8]

Shortly after the first Strategic Arms Limitations agreements were signed, Laird presented Congress with a list of "SALT-related adjustments to strategic programs." Nine programs were to be accelerated because, as then Director of Defense Research and Engineering Dr. John Foster put it, the U.S. must make the SALT accords work by remaining powerful and by having a "timely and credible hedge" against those agreements expiring or being abrogated."[9]

In August of that same year a House-Senate conference again defeated administration proposals to improve warhead accuracies. This time, however, the controversy leaked into the papers, but Defense Department spokesman Jerry Friedheim smoothed things over by stressing that the research program was only designed to provide a "hedge" against possible failure to reach a follow-up SALT-2 treaty on offensive nuclear arms once the SALT-I Interim Agreement expired."[10] While disclaiming any determination to seek a first-strike force he conceded that "if you develop the capability to attack hard targets then the option would be there for some future president to determine whether to deploy that capability."[11]

In spite of Friedheim's assurances, it was only nine months later, in May 1973, that Nixon declared in his foreign policy message to Congress that deterrence based on the ability to kill tens of millions of people was "inconsistent with American values." He claimed that a President needed a nuclear strategy that would allow greater flexibility in his choice of options.[12] By mid-1973 Defense Secretary James Schlesinger authorized work to improve missile accuracy, apparently without first obtaining Congressional approval because that approval was not granted until the following year.

On January 10, 1974, Schlesinger stated at an Overseas Writers Association luncheon in Washington, D.C. that "in the pursuit of symmetry we cannot allow the Soviets unilaterally to obtain a counterforce option which we ourselves lack."[13] However illusory that justification, Schlesinger proceeded to discuss the selection of options he deemed necessary. He said "military targets, whether silos or other military targets, are, of course, one of the possible target sets." He went on to suggest that the President and the so-called National Command Authorities had only massive retaliation against Soviet cities as a response option. This statement was *prima facie* false, since contingencies for counterforce responses have always been outlined in the SIOP (the single integrated operational plan, which is the blueprint for thermonuclear war and the most closely guarded document in existence). Nevertheless, those plans were for relatively massive attacks. Schlesinger sought a *limited* nuclear response whereby one or two missiles could be launched against selected military targets. In this way, he argued, the United States could deter a limited nuclear assault by the Russians which otherwise would go unanswered (since the President might not order an all-out attack on Soviet cities that would almost certainly trigger a corresponding attack on the United States).

. . . the only plausible reason for developing a counterforce capability is to acquire the capacity to launch an unanswerable first strike against the Soviet Union.

During Senate hearings on the military budget the following month, Schlesinger was asked if this newly announced limited counterforce policy would have a destabilizing effect on disarmament negotiations. His reply then was: "We have no *announced* counterforce strategy, if by counterforce one infers that one is going to attempt to destroy silos. We have a new targeting doctrine that emphasizes selectivity and flexibility."[14] (Emphasis added.) Semantic quibbling aside, an unannounced policy may nevertheless exist. The real utility of limited nuclear war emerged on May 30, 1975, when Schlesinger finally admitted publicly that the U.S. would consider using nuclear weapons first to stop communist advances such as in Europe and Korea.[15]

The Nixon-Schlesinger targeting doctrine of selectivity and

flexibility was designed to make limited nuclear war appear more acceptable because it sounds more humane to retaliate against military targets than population areas. It is based on the hypothetical case of a limited Soviet attack employing a handful of missiles. But this contingency is unrealistic for two reasons. First, there is no rational motivation for Moscow to launch such an attack. The risk would be high for the initiating country because there would be no assurance that the response would be equally limited. Secondly, even if the retaliation were limited, there is no guarantee that hostilities would end there. The exchanges would likely escalate to total nuclear war, in which case both sides would be devastated. This likelihood of escalation was cogently pointed out by Defense Secretary Harold Brown in early 1978:

None of this potential flexibility changes my view that a full-scale thermonuclear exchange would be an unprecedented disaster for the Soviet Union as well as for the United States. Nor is it at all clear that an initial use of nuclear weapons— however selectively they might be targeted—could be kept from escalating to a full-scale thermonuclear exchange, especially if command-control centers were brought under attack. [16]

It simmers down to the fact that the only plausible reason for developing a counterforce capability is to acquire the capacity to launch an unanswerable first strike against the Soviet Union. Before exploring this shift in nuclear doctrine, let us review the weapons inventory of current U.S. and Soviet strategic arsenals.

The Strategic Triad

To understand the trend in weapons development one should have some knowledge of the "triad" of weapons that make up the strategic nuclear forces of the United States and the Soviet Union. The U.S. arsenal now contains about 10,000 nuclear warheads carried by delivery vehicles stationed on land, at sea, and in the air (See Figure 1). The land leg today contains 1,054 intercontinental ballistic missiles (ICBMs) deeply entrenched in underground silos throughout the United States. Five hundred and fifty of these are Minuteman-3 missiles which carry three individually-targeted warheads (MIRVs).

The Strategic Air Command possesses approximately 349 intercontinental B-52 bombers. [17] In past years each carried four 24-megaton bombs that were delivered by gravity; now in addition to bombs each plane can be loaded with at least twelve

Figure 1
U.S. Strategic Missiles & Bombers (Mid-1979)[9]

Name	Category	Range (Naut. Mi.)	Number Deployed	Warhead Yield	Number of Warheads/ Missiles	Remarks
Titan 2	ICBM	6,300	54	5-10 MT	1	Liquid fuel
Minuteman-2	ICBM	7,000	450	1-2 MT	1	Solid fuel
Minuteman-3	ICBM	7,000	550	170 KT	3 MIRV	Solid fuel Radiation hardening Penetration aids
Polaris A3	SLBM	2,500	160	200 KT 1 MT	3 MRV 1	Solid fuel Penetration aids
Poseidon C3	SLBM	2,500	496	40 KT	10-14 MIRV	Solid fuel Radiation hardening Penetration aids
B-52	Bomber	Inter-continental	349	Bombs plus SRAM missiles (170-200 KT)		8 turbojet/turbofan engines Subsonic

KT = kilotons   MT = megatons

9

nuclear-tipped short-range attack missiles (SRAMs), capable of hitting targets as much as 100 miles away. Later model B-52s can carry up to twenty SRAMs.

In the sea leg of the triad there are 41 ballistic missile submarines, ten armed with the Polaris missile and 31 with Poseidon.[18] Each carries sixteen missiles. The older Polaris missiles are loaded with three 200-kiloton bombs (called multiple reentry vehicles or MRVs) that explode in a triangular pattern—so that if the trajectory shifts a little to one side there will still be at least one bomb close enough to destroy the target. Poseidon missiles carry from ten to fourteen independently-targeted warheads (MIRVs) of 40-kiloton yield each. That means that each of the 31 Poseidon submarines could destroy at least 160 cities with bombs having at least twice the explosive energy that ripped into Hiroshima and Nagasaki.

The Soviet Union also has ICBMs in silos, missile-carrying submarines, and intercontinental bombers (See Figure 2). A comparison of Figures 1 and 2 indicates that while the Soviets out-number the United States in strategic delivery vehicles (i.e., missiles and bombers), the United States leads in the total number of deliverable strategic nuclear bombs (see Figure 3).

Examination of Figure 3 reveals that the U.S. inventory of strategic bombs took a decided upturn in 1970 when MIRV deployment started. Furthermore, the upturn in Soviet warheads five years later suggests a compensatory response to U.S. MIRVs. With the planned deployment of Missile-X (M-X) in the mid-1980s, the predicted U.S. curve swings up steeply; it becomes precipitous with the introduction of operational Trident-2 missiles in the late 1980s. And because the Soviets have not mastered the technology to miniaturize hydrogen bombs, their inventory will not rise as sharply as the U.S. buildup. The simple fact is that even after both countries have fully deployed MIRVs, the U.S. can still put more bombs on smaller missiles than can the U.S.S.R.

This vast array of power does not satisfy the Pentagon. Virtually every leg of the triad is being modernized to enhance America's first-strike capabilities. Before examining these developments in detail, let us consider what constitutes the ability to inflict an unanswerable first strike with nuclear weapons.

A Knockout First Strike

I mentioned earlier that "damage limitation" can also be associated with a first strike. Former Defense Secretary Donald Rumsfeld discussed that topic in the Pentagon's annual "posture

U.S.S.R. Strategic Missiles and Bombers (Mid-1979)[20]

Name	Category	Range (Naut. Mi.)	Number Deployed	Warhead Yield	Number of Warheads	Remarks
SS-9	ICBM	6,500	138	18-25 MT / 4-5 MT	1 / 3 MRV	Liquid fuel
SS-11	ICBM	5,500	720	1-2 MT / 250 KT	1 / 3 MRV	Storable liquid fuel
SS-13	ICBM	4,350	60	1 MT	1	Solid fuel
SS-17	ICBM	5,650	80	600 KT	4 MIRV	Storable liquid fuel. Replacing SS-11s
SS-18	ICBM	6,500	170	18-25 MT / 1½ MT	1 / 10 MIRV	Storable liquid fuel Replacing SS-9s
SS-19	ICBM	5,500	230	800 KT	6 MIRV	Storable liquid fuel. Replacing SS-11s
SS-N-4	SLBM	300	27	1-2 MT	1	Storable liquid fuel. On 9 Golf (diesel) subs*
SS-N-5	SLBM	650	36	1-2 MT	1	Storable liquid fuel On 11 Golf (diesel) subs* and 1 Hotel sub
SS-N-6	SLBM	1,300	496	1 MT / ? KT	1 / 3 MRV	Storable liquid fuel Possibly some MRVs on 31 Yankee subs
SS-N-8	SLBM	4,200	354	1 MT	1	Storable liquid fuel On Delta-1 & -2 subs and 1 Hotel-3 sub
SS-N-17	SLBM	2,500	48	1 MT	1	Solid fuel. Replacing SS-N-6s on Yankee subs
SS-N-18	SLBM	4,300	48	0.2 MT	3 MIRV	Storable liquid fuel Successor to SS-N-8 on Delta sub
Tu-95 (Bear)	Bomber	Intercont.	100			4 turboprop engines Subsonic
Mya-4 (Bison)	Bomber	Intercont.	35			4 turbojet engines Subsonic

3,600 Total Megatonnage

KT = kiloton   MT = megaton   *Golf (diesel) subs not counted in SALT agreements

11

Figure 3
Total Strategic Nuclear Weapons[21]

statement" for Fiscal Year (FY) 1978:

> ... *The most ambitious [damage limiting] strategy dictates a first-strike capability against an enemy's strategic offensive forces which seeks to destroy as much of his megatonnage as possible before it can be brought into play. An enemy's residual retaliation, assumed to be directed against urban-industrial targets, would be blunted still further by a combination of active and passive defenses, including ASW, ABMs, anti-bomber defenses, civil defense, stockpiles of food and other essentials, and even the dispersal and hardening of essential industry.*[22]

With those two sentences Rumsfeld summed up the scenario for a disabling first strike. In this pamphlet I'll delve into the military systems he mentioned. Basically, a first-strike capability would comprise five elements: (1) a space warfare ability to destroy enemy early warning and communications satellites, (2) extremely accurate missiles and bombers to destroy the opponent's missile silos and other land targets, (3) an anti-submarine warfare force able to sink hostile missile-launching subs, (4) a ballistic missile and bomber defense capable of intercepting any surviving enemy missiles or aircraft that are launched in retaliation, and (5) an intricate network of command, control, and communication to coordinate and integrate (1) through (4).

These five topics will be examined in turn.

Space Warfare

Satellites have emerged as the key link in the Pentagon's warmaking capabilities. Without satellites modern defense activities would be impossible. Instantaneous worldwide communication, precise global navigation, reconnaissance, treaty verification, weather prediction, early warning, and a host of other critical military functions all rely on sophisticated spacecraft. As the late General Brown said, "Space is rapidly becoming a strategic arena." Satellites provide the means and data for directing nuclear weapons as well as constituting weapons platforms themselves. In that sense they are critical to an unanswerable first-strike capability.

The campaign to militarize space was led in Congress in the late 1950s by then-Senate Majority Leader Lyndon Johnson. By 1960, only three years after Sputnik, the United States was well on its way toward using space for strategic purposes. The Discoverer series of satellites were developing sensors for space surveillance. The Samos reconnaissance satellite, Transit navigation satellite, and Midas early warning satellite were in advanced development. When Gary Powers' U-2 was shot down over Russia in 1960, the era of aircraft spying came to an end and satellites increasingly took over the reconnaissance function.

In addition to satellite and space programs specifically designed to enhance the Pentagon's disabling first-strike ambitions, many so-called commercial and civilian spacecraft also served military purposes. Seasat, for example, is ostensibly being used by non-military agencies, but its prime function seems to be the observance of sea state conditions for predicting sonar patterns. The Space Shuttle is another example of a supposedly civilian program being used for military purposes: the shuttle will eventually take over all Defense Department space launches, including satellites for early warning, communications, meteorology, navigation, high energy lasers, and space tracking.

Navigation Satellites

Besides helping ships and airplanes find their way around the world, navigation satellites are used to assure the accuracy of weapons; whether by determining the positioning of a submarine prior to SLBM launchings (as Transit does) or by updating a missile's trajectory during flight (as Navstar will do).

The Transit system consists of six satellites in approximately 500-mile high polar orbits. These satellites can position a submarine to within 50 yards, but for the sub to get a reading it must place a four-foot antenna on the ocean's surface for at least three minutes. That, of course, risks exposure, but detection immediately prior to a missile launch may be acceptable.

The Navstar global positioning system is a new Defense Department radio navigation network which will be used by aircraft, ships, artillery, missiles, and other weapons systems. The full system will consist of 24 satellites in a 12,500-mile polar orbit, and Pentagon authorities are considering adding three geosynchronous satellites with signals 100 times as powerful to overcome local jamming environments.

A limited 12-satellite system is planned for 1981 which will provide two-dimensional navigational fixes on the earth's surface. When, in 1985, the full compliment of 24 satellites is functioning, the goal of precise weapons delivery will be achieved; Navstar will then provide accuracies to within 30 feet in all three dimensions, and velocity to within tenths of a foot per second. For obvious reasons, Navstar has been described as one of the most important and far-reaching satellite programs ever undertaken by the Department of Defense.

Reconnaissance Satellites

A variety of spy satellites is currently in use. Civilian programs like Landsat and Skylab have been used for intelligence purposes. An Air Force satellite known as "Big Bird," consisting of a 12-ton orbiting camera, is launched periodically. Samos is another photoreconnaissance satellite. Both Big Bird and Samos orbit at a very low altitude—between 100 and 200 miles above the earth.

The Navy recently launched an ocean surveillance satellite known as NOSS-1 (Naval Ocean Surveillance Satellite) in a 700-mile orbit. It is designed to monitor surface ships and provide targeting data for tactical cruise missiles. Conceivably, it could someday be equipped with a laser tuned to maximum sea water penetration frequency for detecting submarines.

Communications Satellites

The Defense Satellite Communications System (DSCS) will be fully operational by 1978, with six satellites (four active and two on standby) in a 22,000-mile geosynchronous orbit (orbits synchronized to the earth's rotation so that the spacecraft seems to hover over one spot on the globe). Transmitting on super high frequency (SHF), this system will provide high-rate data transmission and secure voice transmission to give the Department of Defense a worldwide network for surveillance, warning, and command-and-control functions. DSCS will also support the Pentagon's Worldwide Military Command and Control System by interconnecting major bases, large Navy ships, and the Advanced Airborne National Command Post.

FLTSATCOM (Fleet Satellite Communication System) is scheduled for launching into geosynchronous orbit in 1977. Its many SHF and UHF (ultra high frequency) channels will provide data transmission and secure voice communication between naval forces at sea and shore stations. FLTSATCOM will also link up with the Air Force Satellite Communication System (AFSATCOM). AFSATCOM provides UHF teletype service for strategic nuclear forces (SAC bombers and ICBM control centers) as well as for ground and airborne command posts.

Early Warning Satellites

Three U.S. early warning satellites (with 2,000 infrared sensors designed to detect missile launches) are in geosynchronous orbit. One satellite is placed over the Indian Ocean to watch for ICBM launches from the Soviet Union. Two others are over the Atlantic and Pacific Oceans to watch for ballistic missiles launched from submarines.

Satellite Tracking

The U.S.S.R. has a comparable compliment of the various satellites. What they lack in quality they try to make up for in numbers. That is why the number of Soviet space launches exceed those of the United States.

Destruction of certain satellites would be necessary in a knockout first strike. Destroying Soviet early warning and communications satellites would temporarily "blind" the Kremlin and significantly hinder transmitting the fire command to Russian missile commanders before their weapons were blown up. And knocking out navigation satellites would make any "residual retaliation" less accurate in destroying targets in the United States. But a prerequisite to destroying satellites is the ability to locate, identify, and track them so that target trajectories can be pre-planned.

U.S. efforts to monitor all objects in space hints at a desire to *control* space and is a subtle indicator of satellite warfare activity.

Actual plans for tracking satellites began two years before Sputnik was launched. In 1959, as a result of the drive to militarize space, the Defense Advanced Research Projects Agency (DARPA), the Navy, and the Air Force started developing a spacetracking network. In 1960 the responsibility was assigned to the North American Air Defense Command (NORAD) along with anti-satellite functions. Today known as the Space Detection and Tracking System (SPADATS), this network is responsible for tracking all orbiting bodies, monitoring Soviet space programs, providing target data for anti-satellite systems, and identifying objects in space. SPADATS is a worldwide tracking network with a nuclear-survivable underground computer center in Cheyenne Mountain, Colorado, which can predict where any satellite will be at any time.

There is abundant evidence that the United States has been interested in satellite warfare for almost two decades. As early as 1959, DARPA investigated manned, maneuverable anti-satellite satellites. The Russians have also been interested in anti-satellite warfare for some time.

Although there are many sensors associated with SPADATS, its main element is the Air Force's Spacetrack system, consisting of powerful Baker-Nunn cameras and tracking radars spread throughout the globe, as well as phased-array radar in Florida. Spacetrack is now undergoing major modifications. The near-term improvement is called the Ground Electro-Optical Deep Space Surveillance System (GEODSS). GEODSS will use low-light-level television cameras to detect and track any new object not stored in its computerized catalog of orbital bodies. There will be five GEODSS stations equally spaced around the globe. A longer term improvement will involve mosaic long-wavelength infrared (LWIR) sensors on satellites in geosynchronous orbit. A 500-pound sensor called the satellite infrared experiment (SIRE) will soon be launched and a space-based detection and tracking system will eventually replace Spacetrack in the mid-1980s. (Mosaic infrared sensors will be discussed further under Ballistic Missile and Bomber Defense.)

Satwar

There is abundant evidence that the United States has been interested in satellite warfare for almost two decades. As early as 1959, DARPA investigated manned, maneuverable anti-satellite satellites. The Russians have also been interested in anti-satellite warfare for some time. (It is interesting to note the semantic difference used by the Pentagon when referring to U.S. or Soviet weapons: Soviet interceptor satellites are always called "killer satellites," while their American counterparts were named SAINT, an acronym for satellite interceptor.) A half-scale prototype of SAINT was reportedly under construction in 1961, with intercept tests scheduled for 1962. In February, 1962, however, a news blackout on military satellites was ordered by the Pentagon, serving to mask Defense Department space activities to this day.

The early SAINT program was apparently halted before actual vehicle construction because of high costs and technical difficulties. Much of the research on co-orbital intercepts was taken over by the Manned Orbital Laboratory program but that, too, met its demise when President Kennedy found that the Air Force was muscling in on what was supposedly a civilian space program. Nevertheless, in 1963 and 1964, then Director of Defense Research and Engineering Dr. Harold Brown (now Secretary of Defense) made brief references to satellite intercept programs. Some analysts have suggested that orbital rendezvous tests during the Apollo flights were part of the SAINT project, but Brown's references to satellite intercepts probably referred to missiles fired from the earth because all three branches of the military got into the act with direct-ascent weapons.

In 1963, Defense Secretary McNamara directed the Army to conduct anti-satellite tests using their Nike-Zeus ABM interceptors on Kwajalein Atoll, the western end of the Pacific Missile Range. Although some tests were made the following year, it is believed that the system was inactive by 1968. In 1964, in the "Early Spring" program, the Navy used modified Polaris missiles launched from submarines to put a fine screen of metal pellets in front of satellites. In the same year, special thrust-augmented Thor missiles were successfully tested by the Air Force. In 1966, these weapons were again tested using a Burner-2 upper stage, which has a precise maneuvering and positioning capability adaptable to satellite rendezvous. This led to an operational anti-satellite system based on Johnston Island in the Pacific, using Thor boosters with Burner-2 upper stages and nuclear warheads. Although use of these weapons would constitute a violation of the Outer Space Treaty, these missiles were apparently kept in

So-called directed-energy weapons will also have application to anti-satellite warfare. Spaceborne high energy (killer) lasers placed in very high orbit would be most efficient in blasting Soviet satellites from the sky in a surgical manner. President Carter has confirmed that the U.S. is developing a laser beam to destroy satellites.

readiness until 1975 and can still be reactivated on six months notice.

Space Intercept Program 922 was first funded in 1967 and employed Thor boosters with Burner-2 upper stages armed with nonnuclear kill devices. The increased accuracy of target-homing warheads allowed using a cloud of metal pellets rather than hydrogen bombs. Speculation has it that ten Thor-Burner-2 launches between 1967 and 1971 used these homing interceptor technology (HIT) warheads. Vought Corporation now has contracts to develop a ground-launched, direct-ascent, non-nuclear anti-satellite system which will use LWIR sensors to home on its target at hypersonic velocity. The Air Force hopes to put this system in production by late 1980.[23]

So-called directed-energy weapons will also have application to anti-satellite warfare. Spaceborne high energy (killer) lasers placed in very high orbit would be most efficient in blasting Soviet satellites from the sky in a surgical manner. President Carter has confirmed that the U.S. is developing a laser beam to destroy satellites.[24] Likewise, beams of subatomic particles are being developed for anti-satellite purposes. (HIT warheads and directed energy weapons will be discussed further under ballistic missile defense.)

Let us turn briefly to Soviet activities in the area of anti-satellite warfare. In spite of early Air Force predictions that the Soviets would have an anti-satellite capability in 1963, they didn't even start testing such devices until the end of the decade. Their first test series ran from October 1968 until December 1971; a second started in February 1976 and is still going on. All of these tests have involved co-orbital intercepts, which involve placing a target satellite in orbit and then launching an interceptor satellite a few days later. Approximately sixteen tests of this system have taken place, with varying degrees of success. Observations indicate that the Soviets have a very limited anti-satellite capability that is confined to certain low orbits. It is so limited that the target satellite can be identified as such before the interceptor is launched, and, since it takes several hours to reach rendezvous, the interceptor could easily be destroyed before it makes the kill. Moreover, their existing weapons would be ineffective against U.S. communications and early warning satellites in deep space. Nor have the Russians demonstrated direct-ascent intercepts or exotic kill schemes despite all the fuss the Pentagon has made about Soviet anti-satellite weaponry. Even the four-hour blinding of a U.S. early warning satellite in 1975 has now been officially attributed to large natural gas fires and not, as reported at the time, to Soviet laser guns.

Counterforce Missiles

The primary requisite for a disabling first strike is a missile force capable of destroying enemy missile silos and other "hard" military targets. What constitutes a counterforce missile? Despite newspaper reports about Soviet superiority in missile payload and numbers of missiles, the United States has a substantial edge in such categories as numbers of warheads, accuracy, and reliability, the attributes which, in the final analysis, most affect the first-strike capability of a missile.[25]

The fact that the United States had a 3:1 superiority in numbers of strategic warheads is one reason the U.S.S.R. was allowed more missiles when the SALT-I Agreement was signed. The U.S. was ahead in this all-important factor because American missiles were being armed with multiple warheads, allowing one missile to strike several different targets simultaneously. Thus by mid-1979, the Soviet Union had 2,542 strategic missiles and bombers compared to 2,059 for the United States. But that advantage is illusory when we consider that United States launchers can deliver approximately 10,000 warheads as compared to only about 5,000 for the U.S.S.R. As noted by John Newhouse, counselor for the Arms Control and Disarmament Agency, "It is difficult to overstate the importance of this kind of advantage; missile warheads (the actual weapon) not missile launchers (the means of delivery) represent the more critical measure of overall strategic power."[26]

Other parameters of a missile's capabilities are also crucial to this assessment. *Throw weight* and *payload* can be used interchangeably. For a missile they are defined as the weight of the actual warhead that is left after the last rocket motor has been separated in flight. The Soviets have a significant advantage in actual pounds of throw weight but, because the United States has made much headway in miniaturization, we use the available throw weight more efficiently. That, combined with other capabilities such as accuracy and reliability, gives the United States the advantage.

Readiness denotes the number of missiles ready to launch at any given time. There are always a certain number out of service for maintenance and other reasons. According to the Center for Defense Information in Washington, D.C., the readiness of U.S. strategic forces is 95 percent, while the corresponding Soviet readiness is only 75 percent.[27] Using the mid-1979 inventory of

ICBMs and submarine-launched ballistic missiles (SLBMs) this adds up to 1,624 of the United States' 1,710 missiles being ready to launch at any given instant while 1,805 of the Soviet's 2,407 would be available. That alone trims away much of the U.S.S.R.'s lead in delivery systems but, according to former Chairman of the Joint Chiefs of Staff, the late General George S. Brown, America's advantage in readiness may be even larger. He stated in 1978 that only 15 percent of Soviet missile submarines operate away from port at any one time, compared to 55 percent for the U.S., thus reducing the number of Soviet SLBMs that are ready to launch at any given time.[28] Furthermore, other reports indicate that the alert rate of Soviet ICBMs is only 30 percent although that is believed to be climbing.[29]

Reliability refers to the percentage of probability that a missile will complete its mission after it has been launched—i.e., the chances that it will work properly. The reliability of U.S. missiles range from 75 to 80 percent. Soviet reliability is somewhat lower; between 65 and 75 percent.[30] It boils down to Russia's best and newest being only as reliable as America's worst and oldest.

The final two measures of strategic power are *megatonnage* and *accuracy*. They are the attributes most directly related to the ability to destroy hard targets and, consequently, the first-strike ability of a missile. In general, the Soviets have bigger bombs, but that is mainly due to their inability to make small and accurate warheads. Soviet warheads, until recently, would miss their mark by as much as 0.7 nautical miles and many would go as wild as 1-2 nautical miles. Some of their newest ICBMs are better with a miss distance of 0.25-0.3 nautical miles.* In contrast, U.S. missiles, before accuracy improvements, could place their warheads within a 0.25 -0.3 nautical-mile-radius circle. Furthermore, U.S. programs are improving that marksmanship even further while the Soviets are scrambling to catch up. (See Figure 4.)

The ability of a weapon to destroy a hard target is known as its *lethality,* and is symbolized by the letter K. Lethality is directly proportional to the two-thirds power of the warhead explosive yield and inversely proportional to the miss distance squared. The miss distance, or accuracy, is expressed as "circular error probability" (CEP), which is the radius of a circle centered on the target in which half the bombs will explode. The resulting equation is:[33]

---

*Pentagon reports say that the Soviet SS-18 has *demonstrated* an accuracy of 0.1 nautical miles. However, the only accuracies demonstrated are test accuracies which are conducted under near-laboratory conditions. These must be extrapolated to expected operational accuracies which are significantly larger.

$$K = \frac{Y^{2/3}}{(CEP)^2}$$

where: K = lethality of warhead.

Y = warhead yield in megatons.

CEP = accuracy in nautical miles.

We can simply say that making the warhead twice as accurate has the same effect as making the bomb eight times as powerful. Looking at it another way, if the miss distance is cut in half, the warhead need only be one-eighth the power and still maintain the same hard target kill capability. Now let us look at a specific example: The Minuteman-2 missile with a 1-megaton warhead and a CEP of 0.3 nautical miles has a lethality of 11. The next generation Minuteman-3 is equipped with three warheads of 170-kilotons (.17-megatons) and the CEP was trimmed to 0.2 nautical miles. The lethality of each warhead calculates out to 7.66, but since there are three of them on each missile, the total lethality is 23. The net effect is that by MIRVing and increasing the accuracy by 33 percent the Air Force was able to double the hard-target kill capability while reducing the total megatonnage 40 percent.

Lethality is then used (along with the reliability of the missile to function properly and the hardness of the target) to calculate the probability of kill (P_k) for each warhead. This is a more complicated equation and is given in Figure 4.

If we compare the P_k column of Figure 4 for ICBMs we can see that each warhead on the existing Minuteman-3 missiles, with their new NS-20 guidance package and 350 kiloton Mark-12A reentry bodies, will be at least twice as good at destroying missile silos as each warhead on the newest family of Soviet ICBMs. None of them, however, would be certain enough of destroying the silos to be considered a first-strike weapon—although Minuteman-3 is approaching it. If Missile-X is deployed, however, it will have a high enough probability of kill to be considered a first-strike weapon.

The same comparison can be made in a more dramatic form with SLBMs. Neither U.S. Poseidon nor Trident-1 missiles come anywhere near having a first-strike capability. The same holds true for all Soviet SLBMs—including the latest SS-N-18. Trident-2 is another story. Therefore, Missile-X and Trident-2 are first-strike missiles that threaten to upset nuclear stability.

Of course, here we are using lethality merely as a quantitative measure of a nation's counterforce potential from ballistic missiles. The probability of killing a specific hard target considers the lethality of each warhead, the number of warheads directed at that specific target, the reliability of the weapons, and the

Figure 4
Counterforce Capability of Ballistic Missiles [19, 20, 21]

U.S.

Missile	Accuracy of Reentry Vehicle (naut. mi.) CEP	Explosive Yield of Warhead (megatons) Y	Lethality Per Reentry Vehicle K	Number of Reentry Vehicles Per Missile	Reliability of Missile (%) g	Probability of Killing Hard Target (% per RV) Pk	Comments
Minuteman-3 ICBM	0.1	0.35	49.7	3 MIRVs	80	54.68	Accuracy Improve. CEP = 600 ft. Mark-12A MIRVs
Missile-X ICBM	0.05	0.35	100.0*	15 MIRVs**	80	79.65	Mark-12A MIRVs CEP = 300 ft.
Missile-X ICBM	0.015	0.075	100.0*	20 MARVs**	80	79.65	75 kiloton MARVs CEP = 90 ft.
Poseidon SLBM	0.3	0.04	1.3	14 MIRVs	80	2.05	No Accuracy Imp. CEP = 1800 ft.
Trident-1 SLBM	0.25	0.1	3.45	8 MIRVs	80	5.35	Without MARVs CEP = 1500 ft.
Trident-2 SLBM	0.05	0.35	100.0*	7 MIRVs	80	79.65	Mark-12A MIRVs CEP = 300 ft.
Trident-2 SLBM	0.015	0.075	100.0*	17 MARVs**	80	79.65	75 kiloton MARVs CEP = 90 ft.

	CEP	Y	K	MIRVs	Pk (%)		Description
U.S.S.R.							
SS-17 ICBM	0.25	0.6***	11.38	4 MIRVs	75	15.62	600 kiloton MIRVs CEP = 1500 ft.
SS-18 ICBM	0.25	1.5***	20.97	10 MIRVs	75	26.88	1.5 megaton MIRVs CEP = 1500 ft.
SS-19 ICBM	0.20	0.8***	21.54	6 MIRVs	75	27.5	800 kiloton MIRVs CEP = 1500 ft.
SS-N-8 SLBM	0.8	1.0	1.56	1	70	2.15	Single warhead
SS-N-18 SLBM	0.5	0.2	1.37	3 MIRVs	70	1.89	Latest Soviet SLBM

$$K = \frac{Y^{2.3}}{(CEP)^2}$$

$$Pk = 1 - e^{-\left[\dfrac{K \bullet g}{2H^{2/3} \bullet (0.19H^{-1} - 0.23H^{-1/2} + 0.68)^{2/3}}\right]}$$

H = Hardness of target/silo (assume 2,000 p.s.i. overpressure)

CEP = Circular Error Probability (accuracy)

*Use the cutoff value for lethality, $K_{max.} = 100$[32]

**SALT-II will limit the maximum number of MIRVs to 10 for ICBMs and 14 for SLBMs.

***Recently it has been reported (*Washington Post*, May 31, 1979, page 1) that the CIA has significantly revised downward its estimates of Soviet warhead yields to 0.6 megatons for the SS-18, and 550 kilotons for the SS-19. These changes would somewhat reduce the estimated lethality of Soviet missiles.

> . . . when the entire picture is laid out, it becomes apparent that the United States is far ahead of the Soviet Union in the ability to attack military targets. And we should remember that achieving a more aggressive counterforce potential is synonymous with moving toward a disarming first-strike potential.

hardness of the target. Pentagon experts are still trying to determine how to include the effect of fratricide (the destructive effect of a nuclear explosive on other incoming warheads) in the counterforce equation.

These figures, however, illustrate how the information released by the Pentagon suggesting Soviet superiority is misleading. For, when the entire picture is laid out, it becomes apparent that the United States is far ahead of the Soviet Union in the ability to attack military targets. And we should remember that achieving a more aggressive counterforce potential is synonymous with moving toward a disarming first-strike potential.

MIRVs and MARVs

Before we consider the new weapons systems being developed, it would be best to discuss some of the more universal sub-systems. Let us start with some basic concepts. The trajectory of a ballistic missile is made up of three segments: powered flight, coast through space, and reentry into the earth's atmosphere. Rocket motors boost the missile into space while starting it on the correct trajectory to the target. Then they burn out and drop off. What remained on early missiles was a hydrogen bomb packaged in a special capsule called the reentry vehicle (RV) or body. The reentry body then went through the second and longest portion of flight, coasting in an arc through space and eventually dropping back down to reenter the earth's atmosphere.

Early missiles flew a preprogrammed trajectory from a given launch point to a selected target. The necessary heading and velocity were obtained during powered flight when the missile could be controlled by swivel nozzles or other means. After the motors burned out, however, the reentry body sped on to the target like a bullet. That is why these missiles are called ballistic.

Later the United States developed multiple individually-targeted reentry vehicles (MIRVs). Several are attached to the front section of the missile, which is called the "bus." They are then covered with the missile nose cone. When the last rocket motor burns out and separates, the nose cone is ejected. What remains is the bus, which goes through the long coast phase, dropping off its lethal passenger for impact at different destinations.

Originally the Pentagon said MIRVs were needed to penetrate Soviet interceptor missiles such as those being stationed around Moscow. By releasing the individual RVs in sequence, it was argued, the warheads would be spaced far enough apart so that one interceptor could destroy no more than one RV; the supply of interceptors would thus soon be exhausted and remaining RVs would destroy the target. *But the real reason for MIRVs was counterforce:* by programming the bus to move sideways rather than in reverse it is possible to aim each RV at a separate target.

Pre-programmed trajectories are accurate enough for destroying cities but, as we have seen, the key to a first strike is precision. One approach to improving accuracy is the stellar inertial guidance (SIG) technology. Once the missile has left the turbulence of the earth's atmosphere SIG takes a reading on the stars or a satellite to update the missile's navigation computer; corrections are then made by the bus before it starts dropping off warheads. In 1969 the United States developed the SIG system which could be refitted into Poseidon missiles as well as used on the first generation Trident missiles. Such accuracy improvements are only needed to destroy hard targets.

A more efficient concept is being designed for the second generation Trident missile (Trident-2) and for Missile-X. It is the "Navstar" satellite global positioning system, which will give true position in three dimensions within 30 feet and actual velocity within tenths of a foot per second. A missile's navigation computers will be updated during the long coast phase and corrections will be made by the bus just before each RV is released. Navstar fixes will do everything SIG does, and do it more precisely, to insure that each body is correctly aligned in three dimensions and velocity for its trajectory. This will give a target CEP of 300 feet.

None of the systems mentioned so far can foresee excursions from the flight path during reentry into the earth's atmosphere— and those deviations can be profound. Uneven erosion or ablation (melting away of the warhead's surface by air friction), wind, air turbulence, rain, and sleet all have their effect on accuracy. To make corrections for these requires the ability to *maneuver* during reentry.

Lockheed Missiles and Space Company began preliminary studies on a simple maneuvering reentry vehicle (MARV) in 1968. It was called the Special Reentry Body or SRB. The SRB had a bent nose to cause the vehicle to fly at a slight angle during reentry. The angle provided aerodynamic lift similar to that produced by the wings on an airplane, but, because of its tremendous speed, the SRB did not need wings. Inside the SRB was a weight that could be moved from side to side; when the weight was in the middle the RV would fly straight but when it moved to one side the combined action of air pressure and gravity would cause the body to roll. The aerodynamic lift would then have a sideways component which caused the SRB to fly in that direction. A rough analogy to this effect is steering a surfboard by shifting the weight of your body. Careful planning of weight shifts causes various maneuvers. These crude aerobatics were said to be necessary to avoid enemy anti-ballistic missiles (ABM) interceptors but, as in the case of MIRVs, the real purpose was counterforce.

In 1970 Lockheed began concept studies for the Mark-500 maneuvering reentry vehicle to be used on Trident missiles. The Mark-500 uses the same bent nose and shifting weights as the SRB, and turned out in fact to be merely a continuation of SRB development. Evasion of interceptors continued to be the ostensible objective but there was an underlying interest in improved accuracy—the kind needed to attack hard military targets in a first strike. Then in 1972 the ABM treaty was signed by the United States and the U.S.S.R., with its limit of only 200 interceptors for each country, and this undercut the evasion argument. Lacking immediate justification, the Mark-500 was temporarily put on the shelf.

It was also in 1972 that Lockheed was awarded the prime contract to develop the first generation Trident missile without competitive bid. To pacify concerned members of Congress, the Trident contract stipulated that a large portion of the work be distributed to subcontractors. Under that provision, the de-emphasized Mark-500 was given to General Electric. GE had started its own RV maneuvering studies several years earlier, with financing from the Advanced Ballistic Reentry Systems (ABRES) program of the Air Force. The GE MARV featured twin flaps on the bottom side. Moving both flaps in the same direction caused the vehicle to pitch up and down; when they worked scissor-fashion, they caused the body to turn. Combinations of the two movements created an interaction which allowed very precise maneuvering.

In January, 1974 Congressman Les Aspin announced that the

Navy was planning to use a MARV on the Trident missile, suggesting a tacit counterforce intent for Trident in violation of official policy. The Defense Department tried to smooth ruffled emotions in Congress by stating that "there is no plan to deploy a MARV on-target *at this time* . . . "[34] (Emphasis added). They went on to claim that the purpose of the Mark-500 program was to develop the basic technology so the United States could go ahead with further development of MARVs in case the ABM Treaty were ever cancelled.

The ABM Treaty was modified in 1974 to allow only 100 defensive interceptors for each country and, actually, the Soviets had deployed no more than the 64 Galosh ABMs around Moscow. In view of that, it made even less sense to develop the Mark-500 for the purpose of evasion. Nevertheless, Vice Admiral R.Y. Kaufman asserted in 1974 that the Mark-500 had been named "Evader" so everyone will know its purpose is to evade enemy interceptors.[35] Since then, the Mark-500 has been flight tested over the Pacific on Minuteman test missiles and on Trident development flights. These test flights are needed to develop a MARV for target accuracy.

The ABRES program is providing the remaining technology required for a precision MARV. Besides developing the flap control system, ABRES is also working on sensors which will be the eyes of a highly accurate maneuvering body called the Precision Guided Reentry Vehicle (PGRV). The PGRV will scan the target area as it approaches, compare what it sees with a previously acquired map stored in its computer, and then make the necessary course corrections to hit directly on-target. In March 1975, the Air Force announced two competitive eight-month studies on the PGRV concept with General Electric and McDonnell Douglas as the principal contractors. Both companies had previously flight tested maneuvering concepts: GE flew large MARVs with flap controls on four different Atlas missile flights, while McDonnell Douglas demonstrated long, low-level maneuvering reentries from two Atlas flights.

By February of 1976 the Pentagon was still claiming that the Mark-500 was intended to evade Soviet ABMs and that the ABRES program was to develop accuracy. Director of Defense Research and Engineering Dr. Malcolm Currie stated to the House Armed Services Committee: "We have our Mark-500 . . . we hope it will discourage the Soviets from deploying their ABM developments . . . Another type of MARV is the terminally homing MARV and has the prime goal of very high accuracy."[36] (Terminal homing means the ability to home-in on the target during the terminal phase of flight.)

29

By the following month the stories had been changed. Navy spokesmen were then telling the Senate that the Mark-500 is a rudimentary MARV intended to out-maneuver anti-*aircraft* missiles which were allegedly being upgraded for use against reentry bodies. The Pentagon charged that the Soviets were improving their surface-to-air missiles (SAMs) for ABM use. It is obvious, however, that a SAM designed to strike down airplanes cruising at not more than mach-2 cannot readily be upgraded to intercept missile warheads bearing down on their target at mach-20—and all in the time required to take a couple breaths. Former Chairman of the Joint Chiefs of Staff General George S. Brown later undercut those fabricated stories in his FY 1978 posture statement when he said: "There is no present indication that the U.S.S.R. has adapted its extensive surface-to-air (SAM) network to ABM defense, nor that it is currently suitable for that role."[37]

Suspicion grows stronger as we again swing our attention to the ABRES program. As the Mark-500's mission has been changed, so has the PGRV's. The ostensible aim of this program has been switched from improving accuracy to evasion of ABM interceptors without sacrificing accuracy.[38] The project's name has also been changed. It is now called the Advanced Maneuvering Reentry Vehicle (AMARV).

The first phase of the PGRV program, an eight-month study of GE and McDonnell Douglas, has been completed and the second phase of PGRV (renamed AMARV) development is now under way. McDonnell Douglas won the contract to build two and possibly three prototypes for flight testing. (This may throw some light on why the ABRES program had its name changed from PGRV to AMARV: it would have been politically difficult to obtain Congressional approval for flight tests of a precision RV because the ABRES vehicle is earmarked for use on Trident-2 and Missile-X, and such a blatant counterforce program would certainly be viewed as destabilizing to SALT negotiations.) The current AMARV body is controlled by twin flaps similar to the GE design. It is supposed to be capable of maneuvering in the upper atmosphere, flying straight for a while, and then performing low altitude maneuvers before striking the target. A new type of guidance system is supposed to put AMARV back on course so it can deliver its nuclear warhead within 300 feet of the target.

What is not well known is that there is a *third* phase to the ABRES maneuvering program. Radar-based sensors are to be installed on the RV so that maneuvers can be made to correct the course for a *no-miss* strike. Although it is implied that these sensors will not be used in the prototype flight tests, the AMARV will be designed to accept them. Then, with maneuvers confined to gentle course corrections rather than severe evasion aerobatics which upset navigation, the AMARV will have the zero-miss accuracy of an aggressive first-strike weapon. That is the type of reentry body planned for future missiles—one which will explode within 90 feet of its target.

Accuracy Improvements to Existing Weapons

Even while the Pentagon works on new types of warheads, it also strives to improve the accuracy of existing weapons. Many of these improvements are intended for the submarine-launched ballistic missile, but the details are clouded with secrecy. More is known about programs to improve the counterforce capability of Minuteman-3 ICBMs. The Command Data Buffer is a computer system that stores trajectory data for numerous targets and allows Air Force programmers to change the targeting of Minuteman-3 missiles in 25 minutes. The entire force of 550 Minuteman-3s can be retargeted in less than ten hours, a task that used to take weeks. Programs known as "Hybrid Explicit" and "Satin 4" increase the computerized target options for ICBMs and speed up the retargeting process. All of these programs are designed to enhance Washington's capacity to order nuclear strikes against selected military targets in the Soviet Union.

The entire Minuteman-3 force has now been equipped with the new NS-20 guidance system which halves the CEP from 1,200 feet to 600. Now the Air Force is replacing the three Mark-12 reentry bodies on 300 Minuteman-3 missiles with Mark-12A MIRVs, which will up the explosive yield of each warhead from 170 to 350 kilotons.

Accuracy improvements may go even further—to the installation of MARVs on Minuteman-3s. In his FY 1975 budget presentation, former Defense Secretary Schlesinger said "we plan to initiate advanced development of a terminally homing guided MARV *for possible retrofit into both ICBMs and SLBMs.* This MARV could give Minuteman-3 a very high accuracy, if such a capability should be needed in the future."[39] (Emphasis added.) Three years later, General Brown indicated that such retrofitting is still being considered when he said: "Improvements in Minuteman-3 accuracy continue to be pursued to assure greater effectiveness per missile. Additional efforts are focusing on a terminally guided maneuvering reentry vehicle."[40]

Pentagon officials have also alluded to a Mark-20 warhead.[41] It was described in the FY 1975 Defense presentation as a part of the five-year plan for Minuteman improvement. First funding was to be sometime in the future, but the exact year was not indicated. Over a quarter-billion dollars was suggested as the "broad planning figure." Air Force officials reported that the Mark-20 would incorporate the technology being developed by ABRES, so this warhead could conceivably be the terminally homing precision MARV alluded to by James Schlesinger and the late General Brown.

The Strategic Air Command's B-52 bombers are also undergoing extensive improvement. Even before work on the B-1 was halted in June 1977, extensive modifications were planned for the B-52s. Before retiring as commander of SAC, General Russel E. Daugherty said that 300 B-52s would be carried on inventory beyond the year 2000.[42]

Many B-52 modifications have already been completed, including extensive structural and wing rework, installation of SRAM racks, installation of electro-optical target-viewing systems, and what is called the "Phase 6 Mod" to improve the electronic countermeasures and warning systems (i.e., systems to confuse enemy radar systems). In addition, technology for a major modernization is now being developed. These improvements are scheduled to be completed on the first planes by mid-1983, and "could extend the effective life of the strategic bombers by fifteen years" while improving "low-altitude penetration capability."[43] This "retrofit" will install advanced radars and control systems that follow the terrain and guide the plane over natural obstacles while traveling at low altitude (i.e., below the level where enemy radars become effective). Although former Defense Secretary Donald Rumsfeld indicated the B-52 would be primarily a cruise missile carrier, those aircraft appear to be destined for more than that—especially now that there will be no B-1. Skimming the ground at 300 feet altitude for hours at a time is *not* the procedure for launching cruise missiles, as we shall soon see. It seems likely that the B-52 bombers will also be used to penetrate hostile territory, whether during nuclear or conventional war.

Trident

Trident is the Navy's new weapon system designed to modernize the sea leg of the nuclear triad. Former Deputy Defense Secretary David Packard directed the Navy to begin full scale development of Trident in September 1971. In February 1973 the Navy announced plans to base Trident in the Pacific Ocean with its home port along the Hood Canal in Puget Sound, near Bangor, Washington. (There are now plans for an East Coast facility at Kings Bay, Georgia.) Construction of the first submarine commenced the following year. Due to production problems and cost overruns, the Trident sub is now scheduled to be operational in 1981—considerably later than originally planned.

The Trident weapon system is composed of many parts, including a new fleet of submarines and two generations of submarine-launched ballistic missiles (SLBMs), Trident-1 and Trident-2. It will feature such quality improvements as maneuvering reentry bodies and, if the Navy gets its way, an exotic communication system.

Existing Poseidon missile submarines displace 8,250 tons of water when submerged, making them slightly heavier than Navy destroyers; Trident subs will displace *more than double* that figure—up to 18,700 tons. This classes them with the Navy's newest strike cruisers. The 560-foot length of Trident can best be comprehended by visualizing two football fields placed end to end. Each of these submarines will carry twenty-four SLBMs, 50% more than Polaris and Poseidon subs.

The actual number of Trident vessels the Navy plans to build has been consistently disguised. For many years the Navy implied to both Congress and the public that it wanted only ten ships. But when, in early 1975, Congressman Floyd Hicks of Washington state forced the House Armed Services Committee to press for a definitive figure, Deputy Chief of Navy Operations Admiral Frank Price Jr., replied: "Right now, Mr. Chairman, our program is for ten submarines. And that is the program for this point in time."[44] These carefully chosen words left the door open for more and, indeed, the Navy announced plans for the eleventh sub in 1976;[45] the twelfth and thirteenth in 1977.[46] Simple arithmetic suggests that by 1992, when the youngest Poseidon submarine reaches the end of its 25-year service life, the Navy will need 30 Trident submarines to maintain its current inventory of 720 SLBMs. Although Navy charts do not show 30 Trident subs (720 launchers) until 1998 (See Figure 5) at the present delivery schedule of one every eight months, there is no assurance that the schedule won't be accelerated. Figure 5 shows that SLBM

Figure 5
SLBM Launchers[47]

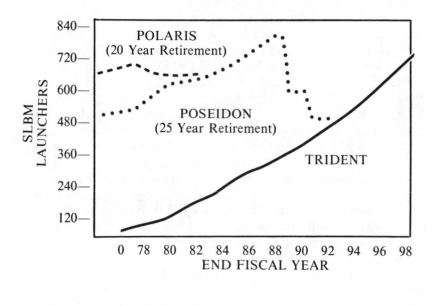

launchers would drop to 480 for several years if the delivery rate isn't stepped up, and it is unlikely that the Navy would tolerate such a contingency in their planning. Defense Department officials are already talking about stretching the service life of Poseidon submarines again—this time to 30 years.

Probably the most important selling point for Trident is that its longer-range missiles will give the submarine ten times as much ocean area in which to hide than that possible with the Poseidon system. Two generations of Trident missiles are planned: Trident-1 will be the same size as the Poseidon missile— 34 feet long and 74 inches diameter—but will weigh 70,000 pounds, a ton heavier. Its projected range is 4,000 nautical miles (with a full load of eight 100-kiloton warheads), and it is as accurate as Poseidon is at 2,000. That, presumably, would make Trident much more accurate when fired at Poseidon's shorter range. Besides being loaded on the new submarines, Trident-1 will also be backfitted into 12 (present plan) Poseidon subs starting in 1979.

The principal means of obtaining more range for the Trident-1 is to use the center space under the nose cone (occupied by four reentry bodies on Poseidon) to mount a small third stage rocket motor. Trident-1 also takes advantage of lighter composite structural material, electronics micro-miniaturization, lightweight motor cases, and a new high energy propellant. But monumental failures trying to implement these technologies[48] has set the Trident-1 missile flight test program over a year behind schedule.

Initial funding for the Trident-2 missile was refused by Congress for fiscal years 1976 and 1977. $5 million was appropriated for concept studies during 1978 and the funding curve has turned steeply upward since then. The range goal for the Trident-2 missile with a full payload was originally 6,000 nautical miles but current Trident-1 problems will certainly be reflected in Trident-2's performance. Some reports now refer to it as a 4,500 nautical mile missile. Trident-2 is due to become operational during the latter 1980s and at 42 feet in length and 83 inches in diameter, it will fit only into the new submarines.

To illustrate the potential destructiveness of the Trident system, consider that each Trident submarine will be equipped with 24 Trident-2 missiles capable of striking any point on over half the earth's surface. Each missile can deliver seventeen superaccurate MARV warheads to within a few feet of as many targets.* With a typical payload of 75-100 kilotons per warhead, that means one Trident submarine will be able to destroy 408 cities or military targets with a blast five times that which was unleashed over Hiroshima. A fleet of thirty Trident submarines would be able to deliver an unbelievable 12,240 nuclear warheads against an enemy's territory—or 30 times the number originally thought sufficient for strategic deterrence. Clearly, if Trident attains the accuracies the Navy seeks, it will constitute the ultimate first-strike weapon.

Trident is so deadly that the *Fiscal Year 1980 Arms Control Impact Statements* (a report the President is required to submit to Congress along with the military budget) described it thus:

> *The addition of highly accurate Trident-2 missiles with higher yield warheads would give U.S. SLBM forces a substantial time-urgent hard-target-kill capability for a first-strike . . .*
>
> *. . . the countersilo capability of a [deleted] KT Trident-2 missile would exceed that of all currently deployed U.S. ballistic missiles. Moreover, the additional effects of two*

---

*If ratified, SALT II, which expires in 1985, will limit each missile to fourteen warheads or 336 warheads in each Trident submarine.

potential advances (Trident-2 and M-X) in U.S. countersilo capabilities by the early 1990s could put a large portion of Soviet fixed ICBM silos at risk. This could have significant destabilizing effects . . . [49]

Missile-X

Incredible pressure was put on President Carter to deploy huge mobile M-X (Missile-X) missiles to offset the nuclear might supposedly lost when he terminated the B-1 bomber program. Less than a week after the B-1 cancellation, Paul H. Nitze, policy chairman for the Committee on the Present Danger (an ultra-conservative group founded by 141 leaders in the military-industrial-academic complex to combat any softness toward the Soviet threat) said in a press conference that the M-X may well be the next critical issue in the arms debate. That prediction has come true and the M-X today is fiercely debated.

The Strategic Exercise (Strat-X) study launched in 1966 looked at various basing modes for U.S. strategic weapons. Over $120 million was spent to define a successor for Minuteman and Titan ICBMs prior to initiation of the Missile-X program in 1972. Although as many as 95 percent of present U.S. silo-based ICBMs are predicted to survive nuclear attack, Pentagon officials claim that they will become vulnerable to Soviet ICBMs in the 1980s. Just before his resignation as Defense Secretary in 1977, Donald Rumsfeld warned: "Our calculations indicate that by the early 1980s there could be a substantial reduction in the number of surviving ICBMs should the Soviets apply sufficient numbers of their forces against the U.S. ICBM force in a first strike."[50] With that collection of suppositions he asked for $294 million to put Missile-X into the final stages of development and testing to make the weapon operational by 1983, two years ahead of previous plans. After originally rejecting the Rumsfeld proposal, the Carter Administration decided in October 1977 to proceed with full-scale development of the M-X. That decision was later reversed and the reversal held in 1978. However, in 1979 the Administration asked to put M-X into full scale development without defining the basing details. It appears that this move is offered to pacify some hawkish Senators into ratifying the SALT-II Treaty.

In 1974, the Missile-X program was looking at thirteen land-mobile concepts, including missile pods in the bottom of ponds, truck- and rail-borne capsules, and trenches. Air mobility was also considered, and in that year the Air Force actually launched a Minuteman missile from a C-5A transport over the Pacific

Ocean to prove its feasibility. By early 1977 the basing concepts had narrowed to three—air-mobile, trenches, and shelters—and in October Defense Secretary Brown announced that the Pentagon would go ahead with a trench system.

Shortly thereafter, a study by Massachusetts Institute of Technology scientists disclosed that mobile missiles in trenches hardened to only 300 p.s.i. overpressure were more vulnerable than present Minuteman missiles in silos. So the Air Force came up with a scheme for hiding each M-X among 20-28 silos. This ran into trouble with the Administration because silos had always been equated with launchers, and launcher numbers were limited by SALT. In return, the Administration started showing interest in air-mobility—possibly because such a basing mode would be less visible and thereby escape the political and environmental effects anticipated when large areas of land are closed off and dug up. In fact, an air-to-surface ballistic missile (ASBM) is allowed in the SALT-II accord.

The Air Force, however, has now conceived of a *racetrack* system of 200 closed-loop roads in the southwestern United States. Each road will have 20-25 spurs leading to as many *bunkers* into which an MX missile can be shuttled. These bunkers will be about 7,000 feet apart.

Missile-X raises critical arms control questions. A basic tenet of any treaty is that compliance with the agreement be verified by each side. Satellites can monitor trenches and shelters as well as silos, but in the past it has always been assumed that each silo contains a missile. The Air Force has proposed several plans for allowing verification of the number of missiles deployed under the race track scheme. But because extra missiles could always be concealed in the bunkers, verification presents serious difficulties and the problem will become more acute when the Soviets react to make their missiles mobile.

Although the SALT-I Interim Agreement on Offense Weapons did not explicitly prohibit the development of mobile strategic missiles, the United States had signed a unilateral statement that it "would consider the deployment of operational land-mobile launchers . . . as inconsistent with the objectives of the Agreement."[51] Now the United States is, itself, moving toward such a system. Since the generally accepted motive of the SALT-I accords was to insure each country the ability to inflict unacceptable retaliation if attacked, we can only assume that the Pentagon's intention regarding Missile-X is inconsistent with allowing the Soviet Union to have that deterrent capability. Here is another indication that the Pentagon is seeking the ability to inflict a disabling first-strike.

> The M-X will sport a new guidance system known as the advanced inertial reference sphere (AIRS) which will provide midcourse positioning to within 100 feet—giving a target CEP of 600 feet. Later, when supplemented by Navstar, the midcourse error will be cut to 30 feet and the target CEP to 300 feet.

Even more salient in this regard are the characteristics of Missile-X itself. The Pentagon describes it as an advanced, high throw-weight MIRVed ICBM capable of fulfilling our strategic requirements into the 21st century. It will be a four-stage missile measuring 92 inches diameter and 70½ feet in length, weighing 95 tons (190,000 pounds), and boosting a payload of at least 4½ tons over a range of 7,000 miles. The M-X will sport a new guidance system known as the advanced inertial reference sphere (AIRS) which will provide midcourse positioning to within 100 feet— giving a target CEP of 600 feet. Later, when supplemented by Navstar, the midcourse error will be cut to 30 feet and the target CEP to 300 feet.

The initial reentry body for Missile-X is the Mark-12A warhead discussed earlier in the description of Minuteman-3 missiles. Air Force spokesmen however, refer to a new M-X warhead which cannot be retrofitted on the Minuteman-3. Since the Pentagon has always left the door open for a target-homing MARV on its new missile, we must suspect that that is what they are talking about. At least twenty precision-guided MARVs in the 75-100 kiloton range could be carried by the M-X.* Missile-X thus fits the pattern of the type of precise weapon being developed to support a first-strike counterforce policy. Indeed, Frank Barnaby of the Stockholm International Peace Research Institute warns that deployment of Missile-X will probably "provoke the Soviet Union to deploy even larger and more numerous warheads to threaten all possible M-X sites."[52] And Brookings Institution arms control specialist John Baker describes Missile-X as "the most crucial arms control issue to be examined in the next five years."[53] The President's arms control impact statement says:

---

*SALT-II would limit the number to ten.

... if the M-X were deployed in substantial numbers, the U.S. would have acquired, through both the Minuteman and M-X programs, an apparent capability to destroy most of the Soviet silo-based ICBM force in a first-strike.[54]

... under crisis conditions, Soviet leaders, concerned that war was imminent, and fearing for the survival of their ICBMs if the United States struck first, nonetheless might perceive pressures to strike first themselves. Such a situation, of course, would be unstable.[55]

Cruise Missiles

Rapidly gaining popularity in military circles and blessed by President Carter since he cancelled the B-1 bomber, the cruise missile is nothing more than a small, pilotless jet airplane which is programmed to fly a prescribed route and then to crash into its intended target. As an air-breathing vehicle, the cruise is limited to operating in the lower atmosphere where it can scoop up air to mix with fuel for combustion (as contrasted to an ICBM's rocket motor, which contains its own fuel and oxidizer).

Three types of small, long-range cruise missiles are currently under development in the United States: the air-launched cruise missile (ALCM) being developed by the Air Force, the sea-launched cruise missile (SLCM) being developed by the Navy, and the ground-launched cruise missile (GLCM) which is a derivative of the SLCM. They all use the same warhead and are propelled by the same fanjet engine (30 inches long by 12 inches diameter and weighing 126 pounds). The common warhead is a 200-kiloton bomb that was developed for a new SRAM-B missile designed for the B-1 bomber. Also common to all three, although not packaged in exactly the same shape, is the missile's navigation system. It consists of an automatic pilot controlled by an inertial guidance platform, which in turn is periodically updated by a sensor system called TERCOM (terrain contour matching).

TERCOM is the device that steers cruise missiles to their targets with such deadly accuracy that they have almost 100 percent "kill capacity" against hardened emplacements. It compares the ground below with a map of the target route stored in its computer; when it deviates from its course a correctional signal is sent to the guidance package which orders corrective maneuvers. TERCOM also allows the missile to skim the ground so low that detection by radar is virtually impossible, while at the same time hedge-hopping over and around any obstacles in its path.

The Air Force started its air-launched version in 1973, about a year after the Navy began work on a cruise missile. The ALCM-A is 14 feet long, has a 25-inch noncircular cross section, weighs about 1,800 pounds and is designed to fit the SRAM racks of the B-52 bomber. The B-52 has one rack (capable of holding eight missiles), plus twelve underwing pylons which make a total capacity of twenty ALCMs.

ALCM-A's have a range of 650 nautical miles when flying the "high-low profile," a technique requiring the missile to stay high until it reaches enemy territory, and then to drop to a low altitude where it can evade radar defenses. (Like airplanes, cruise missiles get best fuel economy at high altitudes but are easier to detect there; when they go lower they sacrifice range for survivability.) For the high-low profile, the ALCM is released from a bomber at 45,000 feet. Within two seconds the wings and tail are unfolded and the engine is running. It travels at mach-0.55 most of the way. Approaching hostile territory, it descends to within 100 feet of the surface to follow hills and valleys. Fifty miles from its target it drops to a mere fifty feet off the ground and speeds up to mach-0.7 for its final dash.

The 20½-foot long sea-launched cruise missile, recently dubbed Tomahawk, is designed to fit the 21-inch diameter torpedo tubes of U.S. nuclear-powered submarines. It will also be carried aboard nuclear-powered strike cruisers. This means that cruise missiles will give attack submarines and cruisers a strategic role. Actually, however, any surface ship can be equipped to launch the versatile SLCMs, which are presently scheduled to be operational in 1980.

The first Tomahawks will burn a fuel known as TH-Dimer which would permit them to achieve a 2,100 nautical mile range when flying a high-low profile (SALT-II prohibits deployment of SLCMs with a range greater than 600 Km, or 326 nautical miles, until the protocol to the treaty expires in 1983). Chemists are working on an even more advanced fuel, called Shelldyne-H, which is twenty percent more concentrated and would stretch the SLCM's range to at least 2,500 nautical miles, matching Polaris and Poseidon ballistic missiles.

The high-low profile for Tomahawk is not quite the same as for the ALCMs, as a three-foot long rocket motor is required to boost the missile skyward for the high part of the profile. The launch from a submarine, therefore, follows a different sequence. After the SLCM is ejected from the torpedo tube, its rocket motor ignites underwater and a swivel nozzle tips the missile upward to broach the surface. Tail fins unfold as the rocket motors continues to shoot skyward. When the booster burns out and separates, the wings unfold as the fanjet engine lights up. The SLCM continues to climb to about 20,000 feet where it cruises until it nears enemy territory. Then it drops close to the ground and continues to the target in much the same manner as the air-launched version.

A 300-mile tactical SLCM with a conventional explosive warhead is propelled by a cheaper but less efficient turbojet engine and uses a modified Harpoon missile guidance system. Both tactical and strategic SLCMs look identical from the outside and they are launched in the same manner from the same launchers. There is no unique manner in which one can be distinguished from the other as far as treaty verification is concerned.

The Navy has also developed an air-launched variant of the Tomahawk for its carrier-based aircraft and is competing with the Air Force for the strategic ALCM. Since the booster rocket is not needed for air launch, the length of Tomahawk is reduced to 18¼ feet. Also, the air-launched Tomahawk burns a less concentrated jet fuel which reduces its range to 1,600 nautical miles for the high-low profile. Up to 60 Tomahawks could be carried abroad modified wide-bodied jetliners such as the 747 and DC-10. If the SRAM rack were removed from the B-52, nine Tomahawks would fit in each bomb bay with another twelve under the wings. The Navy has also proposed a cut-down version of Tomahawk that will fit the existing SRAM racks.

The Navy's versatile Tomahawk was chosen as the candidate for a rocket-assisted ground-launched cruise missile (GLCM), mainly because it already had a booster motor design. Although the GLCM is a joint effort under the auspices of the Air Force, it will join the ALCM and SLCM under the Joint Services Cruise Missile Program Office managed by the Navy.

Not to be outdone, the Air Force has now started on a B-version of its ALCM. The modified version will double the ALCM-A's 650 nautical mile range by adding a five-foot long section in the fuselage to hold the additional fuel. The ALCM-B will still fit the rotary racks of the B-52. It would not have gone through the smaller bomb bay doors of the B-1 but that is no longer a consideration. Competitive flyoffs to choose between the Tomahawk and ALCM-B for a strategic nuclear mission are scheduled for September 1979.

It is only a matter of time before the Army demands *its* share of the cruise missile program. Indeed, NATO planners are already contemplating the possibility of using ground-launched cruise missiles with nuclear warheads to replace some of their shorter range ballistic missiles. GLCMs fired from mobile launchers

41

anywhere in Western Europe would be able to reach all of Russia lying west of the Ural Mountains, threatening forty percent of the Soviet population and most of their industry.

It is too soon to know how many GLCMs the Pentagon intends to acquire, but the Air Force intends to buy 2,328 ALCMs and the Navy plans to put 1,200 Tomahawks on strike cruisers, attack subs, and ballistic missile submarines. Even these preliminary figures indicate why the Soviets are concerned about this prolific new weapon. Cruise missiles would be able to approach their homeland from so many directions that defense against them would require a terrific investment.*

If we look further into the future it is possible to see the realization of still more Air Force dreams. A new bomber-launched weapon called the advanced strategic air-launched missile (ASALM) is now in the advanced stages of development. Capable of skimming the ground at supersonic speeds over long distances, it is being advertised as a weapon to compliment and eventually replace SRAMs. Government officials have made it clear that they don't want ASALM confused with cruise missiles (presumably because it would complicate SALT negotiations), but when the ASALM is finally unveiled we will see that it is nothing more than a cruise missile with supersonic capability. Indeed, Pentagon officials admit that if ASALM were available now it would be the preferred weapon. The ASALM program has recently been speeded up by two years. ASALM is now scheduled to enter full scale development in late 1981 with initial operation of the weapon in 1985. Clearly, cruise missiles are just the beginning of a long line of lethal and destabilizing weapons.

Penetrating Bombers

Regardless of the extensive cruise missile programs and the B-52 modifications discussed earlier, continued Air Force interest

---

*The Soviets also have cruise missiles, but only about 400 of them can go farther than 70 miles. Those are the SS-N-3 "Shaddocks" which can fly 500 nautical miles, but are limited by their guidance capabilities to 250 nautical miles. About 200 of the 42-foot long Shaddocks are carried in "Echo-2" submarines, old vessels which have already used up most of their service life. When the SALT-I agreements were signed in 1972, U.S. officials assigned little strategic importance to Shaddocks and Echo-2 subs. They weren't even counted against Russia's quota of missile-launching submarines. Given America's anti-submarine warfare capabilities (which we shall discuss later) and the fact that Echo-2 boats must surface to launch their missiles and that those missiles require support aircraft for accuracy, it is inconceivable that Soviet cruise missiles could threaten the U.S. coastline. The Soviets are allegedly developing a follow-on to the Shaddock—the SS-NX-12 with an effective range of about 300 nautical miles—but there is no evidence that they are building new cruise missile submarines.

in retaining a penetrating bomber capability (i.e., a bomber capable of overcoming Soviet air defenses and penetrating enemy air space), caused the Pentagon and Congress to consider alternatives to the terminated B-1. Toward the end of 1977, the Senate Armed Services Committee voted a $20 million addition to the fiscal 1978 budget for the purpose of studying an advanced FB-111 strategic bomber. The proposed version, designated the FB-111H, would be stretched longer and equipped with the more powerful B-1 bomber engines. As events unfolded, however, it became apparent that the FB-111 modification wasn't a new idea. Evidently the Pentagon has been discussing the concept with General Dynamics, the FB-111 builder, for almost three years, and that company has spent $10 million of "discretionary funds" to subject scale models to wind tunnel testing over the past two years.

There are presently 68 FB-111As in the Strategic Air Command's inventory, although the aircraft is not supposed to be a strategic aircraft. The present plan calls for converting two of them to the "H" configuration as test planes. Once those have been successfully tested, 65 more of the existing aircraft would be modified while at the same time production lines would be reopened to turn out 100 new FB-111Hs. Total cost for the proposed fleet of 167 aircraft is estimated at $7 billion. Although there have been no funds requested in recent years to proceed with the FB-111H concept, testimony indicates that the Air Force is still keeping the option open.

Meanwhile, Rockwell International is exerting heavy pressure on Congress to continue funding the B-1 program. The company has released extensive proposals on how the B-1 could fill the role of a cruise missile carrier. Rockwell has come up with schemes showing that the B-1 could carry as many as thirty full-length ALCM-Bs—sixteen internally, eight under the wings, and another six beneath the fuselage body.

The B-1/FB-111H debate is not the end of the bomber issue. The Senate Armed Services Committee urged the Pentagon to start investigating a *new* penetrating bomber to replace the B-52s and the FB-111s in the 1990s. The committee approved $5 million for preliminary studies of the new aircraft, dubbed B-X.

Although B-X was soundly defeated in October 1977, the National Aeronautics and Space Administration (NASA) released a contract the following month for Lockheed Corporation to study a new transport aircraft—supposedly civilian— which the Air Force had been interested in for several years previous. This hypersonic aircraft would burn hydrogen fuel to cruise at 4,000 miles per hour at the unprecedented altitude of

125,000 feet.[56]

Also in November 1977, Defense Under Secretary for Research and Engineering, Dr. William J. Perry, announced that his office planned to contract aerospace firms to study the role of a strategic penetrating bomber. That study was completed in August 1978 but Dr. Perry requested another $10 million to analyze specific approaches during 1979.

Meanwhile, the Air Force has been conducting research on its own. By early 1978 it had completed an exercise called SABER PENETRATOR VII aimed at "addressing strategic bomber weapons mix alternatives for the mid-1980s."[57] Strategic Air Commander, General Richard H. Ellis, said the $10 million requested by Dr. Perry is only the first phase of studying a completely different aircraft. "It might turn out to be the B-2 if anything ever develops from it," he explained, "but it would be many steps beyond the B-1."[58]

These studies have also brought Boeing and McDonnell Douglas into the act. They have submitted designs ranging from the flying wing concept to an aircraft which would fold its wings completely away and fly like a rocket ship. The trend now seems to be toward very-fast and very-high-flying penetrators—higher and faster than current Soviet systems can defend against.

The idea of a penetrating bomber for the strategic triad is not dead. Development of a new intercontinental heavy bomber will possibly begin in late 1982.[59]

Anti-Submarine Warfare

In order to launch a nuclear first strike against the U.S.S.R., without incurring unacceptable retaliation, it would be necessary to simultaneously destroy all Soviet missile-carrying submarines. It has been the alleged inability of any nation to pinpoint and destroy all opposing missile submarines that is consistently proferred as the reason an unanswerable first strike is impossible. Even President Carter has stated that "There would be no possibility under the sun that a first-strike capability would be adequate . . . There is no way to prevent a massive retaliatory strike because for all practical purposes atomic submarines are invulnerable."[60] Nevertheless, the Department of Defense spends billions of dollars every year on anti-submarine warfare (ASW), to say nothing about the unknown amounts spent for this purpose by such agencies as the Energy Research and Development Administration, the National Aeronautics and Space Administration, and the National Science Foundation. ASW is no longer just defense against hostile submarines; it is an aggressive activity.

To better understand the entire picture, let us review the number of Soviet submarines that would have to be instantaneously destroyed. In mid-1979 the U.S.S.R. had about sixty-four nuclear-powered ballistic missile submarines.[61] Let us say that by the mid-1980s the Soviets will have between seventy-five and eighty SSBNs capable of running submerged for extended periods. That number should pose no problem for the techniques the U.S. is developing. And the job of destroying them is made easier by the fact that only about fifteen percent are away from port at any time. Most could be hit in their pens.

Anti-submarine warfare systems can be divided into three main components: sensors, to locate and track enemy subs; weapons, to destroy them; and platforms, to carry the sensors and weapons. We will look at all three in turn.

ASW Sensors

Sensors are the eyes and ears of ASW, and have the function of detecting, tracking, and classifying submarines. That task is further broken down into escort and area surveillance. Escort surveillance, as the name implies, is ostensibly to protect convoys and task forces from enemy hunter-killer subs. It is concentrated in a small piece of ocean not more than 60 miles around the ships. The types of sensors used are designed to pinpoint a submarine in that area and determine if it is hostile. Area surveillance, on the other hand, is ocean-wide. Its purpose is to track all submarines and to pinpoint their location within a 60-mile radius (where escort surveillance takes over). It is obvious how these two types of surveillance would have to complement each other if a nation were considering simultaneous destruction of an opponent's entire subsurface fleet.

Sound has always been the most effective means of undersea sensing because radio-type waves will not travel through water. Sound travels for thousands of miles through the ocean but it bends as it zips along much as light is refracted as it passes through a lens. Sound also bounces off the ocean surface and bottom so that it is scattered into multiple paths and zig-zag patterns. The warmer layer of water near the surface (called the thermal layers) also reflect sounds from below back down into the depths. To further complicate matters, sea creatures, ships, storms, rumbling volcanoes, and other phenomena all add to the cacophony of the depths.

Devices used to detect the sounds made by submarines are called sonars. Passive sonars only listen and thus can remain undetected for long periods of time. Active sonars emit sounds which bounce back from submarines or other objects; they are vulnerable to enemy countermeasures unless well protected, and are not suitable for clandestine operations.

To put ASW aircraft and ships within 60 miles of every Russian submarine is the function of *area surveillance*. SOSUS (sound surveillance system) is the backbone of the Navy's ocean-wide undersea sensing apparatus. Although over twenty years old, it has been continuously upgraded. SOSUS is currently undergoing a two-phased improvement program intended to integrate all the surveillance sensor systems into a fully coordinated and centrally located network.

SOSUS is composed of fixed, passive hydrophones (underwater listening devices) located on the continental shelves throughout the oceans of the world. The general location of some of these installations is common knowledge. The sonar chain between Greenland and Scotland detects every Soviet submarine entering the North Atlantic from the Arctic Ocean. The Azores Fixed Acoustic Range monitors submarine traffic through the Strait of Gibraltar and adjacent waters. These are two of the many sonar locations which, when conditions are favorable, can detect and locate a hostile submarine anywhere in the world. SOSUS does, however, have limitations, so the Navy is developing two augmenting systems: towed arrays and moored arrays.

Towed arrays are sonar devices that are pulled around the oceans by slow, fishing-boat type vessels. By relaying acoustic data via satellite to shore stations for processing and analysis, towed area surveillance arrays provide a geographic flexibility which SOSUS does not have. Moored arrays, as described by the Navy, are sonar buoys deployed by submarine, ship, or aircraft throughout a given area of interest. They can be rapidly introduced into a crisis area to augment existing systems. Moored arrays were scheduled to go into final development in 1977, but the Navy abruptly delayed that step a few years. The unadmitted reason appears to be a breakthrough in sonar technology by the Defense Advanced Research Projects Agency (DARPA).

DARPA's interest in underwater sound patterns started by towing a sonar array around the ocean when, contrary to previous belief, they found it was possible to predict sound travel from one time and space to another. Although underwater sound conditions are constantly changing, they do remain fixed for brief periods of time and thus, by examining a series of short time slices, the ocean becomes a predictable sound medium. DARPA sought to exploit this principle in 1973, when, as part of the Navy's Long-Range Propagation Project, it used the array to make measurements at sea that could be used to develop a computer program that would predict ambient oceanic noise. It seemed more than coincidence when, during the Eighth International Acoustics Congress in London a year later, a representative from Bell Laboratories delivered a paper describing a computer simulation that predicts underwater sound patterns by combining known oceanographic information with current sea state data.[62] When the resulting prediction is compared with actual sonar readings, the background noise can be cancelled out to allow isolation of hostile submarines.

Thermal layers, ocean floor contours, and surface choppiness all contribute to the bending, bouncing, and scattering of sound. The resulting zig-zag path has a bearing on how long it takes sound to travel from any given source to a sensing system. Bottom contours and coastline irregularities are easy to plug into a computer model, because they are known and remain constant, but sea state samples must be obtained by satellite and introduced into the calculations at half-mile intervals. The resulting simulation provides an updated picture, in two minutes of computer time, for sound propagation over a 10,000-mile range. The Bell simulation can reportedly pinpoint a submarine within ten miles at that distance.

Early in 1975 DARPA announced a new program called Project Seaguard which is designed to combine the peak performance of acoustic arrays with a network of data-processing stations to achieve optimum detection, location, and tracking accuracies for very quiet submarines. Seaguard will arrange combinations of mobile and fixed arrays that can triangulate on potential targets and provide all essential data—

DARPA has . . . developed the Illiac-4, one of the world's most powerful computers. It operates as if 64 identical computers were working in parallel, which vastly increases the volume of data that can be processed at any given time.

---

identity, location, direction of travel in "real time" (i.e., in time to mount an effective military response). All this data must be received and processed instantly, which requires a computer capacity far exceeding conventional units. DARPA has therefore developed the Illiac-4, one of the world's most powerful computers. It operates as if 64 identical computers were working in parallel, which vastly increases the volume of data that can be processed at any given time. Seaguard could become fully operational in 1982.

A spectrum of spacecraft, including ocean surveillance satellites, will collect meteorological and oceanographic data required for such computer operations. Most prominent is the new Seasat ocean dynamics satellite. Although the first Seasat failed early in its orbital life, these spacecraft contain more sensors than any other satellite. Each satellite will provide the equivalent of 20,000 daily weather reports from ships and land stations around the globe. It will provide day and night observations in almost any weather of: wind velocities and direction; height, shape and length of waves; precise sea surface topography due to currents, tides and storms; gravity-related depressions in the ocean's surface; and oceanic current patterns, surface temperature, and ice packs. All of this information is needed to predict sound propagation patterns.

A constellation of six operational satellites will eventually be put in polar orbit for use between 1985 and the end of the century. Using the Navstar global positioning system to establish their readings within 30 feet, those six satellites will update this weather data over 95 percent of the earth's surface every six hours. That seems to be a small enough time slice for timely computer predictions. The new Seaguard project should then allow the Navy to keep track of every Soviet submarine.

A new type of ASW sensor now under development is the optical ranging, identification and communications system (ORICS), a laser that operates in the blue-green wavelength of the visible light spectrum, which is the optimum tuning for sea water penetration. ORICS will have military ASW application in a few years, and is also being considered for communication with friendly submarines. ASW helicopters equipped with ORICS have already proved successful in locating submarines off the Florida keys. Thus this new technology opens speculation on a more encompassing area surveillance system.

In the mid-1960s, DARPA conducted the Deep Look program aimed at overcoming some fundamental problems in light travel through the ocean. The goal of the exercise was to determine the physical limits to underwater imaging and then to develop new technologies permitting maximum penetration. Two space programs appear to be connected to this effort. The first earth resources satellite, known as Landsat, is advertised as an instrument to combat global food and energy shortages by monitoring crop growth, but has also photographed scenes of military significance such as the Soviet missiles facilities at Kapustin Yar and Plesetsk. Skylab was also used for military purposes. Such satellites scan the earth with a variety of color frequencies, and some of their photos, taken close to the wavelength of maximum water penetration, reveal the ocean bottom in shallow coastal areas. Today the Navy is spending a large share of its research and development funds on improving the ocean-penetrating capabilities of Landsat's multi-spectral cameras.

There seem to be other, later developments which are not being advertised. According to a source in the satellite communication field, the U.S. Navy has been experimenting with short-duration laser satellites for photographing the ocean floor, again using the blue-green frequency to null out sea water. Apparently the project was successful, and such photographs are now considered within U.S. technical capabilities. And, if the ocean bottom can be photographed, it should also be possible to photograph submarines that happen to be in the vicinity. Going a step further, the laser could then be used for continuous surveillance of enemy subs, or for very accurate pinpointing and identification.

Once the general location of a hostile submarine is known, it is the job of *escort surveillance* to determine its precise location. Hull-mounted sonars are the oldest means of escort surveillance. They are huge devices mounted below the water-line in the bows of ships and submarines. Each sonar contains thousands of individual sensors which provide a variety of active and passive modes over various ranges. Sonar arrays towed behind ships supplement hull-mounted sonars, but they are long and awkward to handle. Existing types must be towed slowly or the self-generated noise will mask the sounds they are supposed to detect. They also slow the ship down in emergencies, but a new type, scheduled for operation in 1980, will alleviate those problems as well as provide more sensitivity. Regardless of improvements, however, both hull-mounted and towed sonars are limited by the thermal layers; if the noise from submarines is bounced back down they cannot be detected from the surface. For that reason a variable-depth sonar has been developed that plunges below the thermal layers. Towed by a 600-foot cable and stabilized by a gyro as it "flys" deep through the water, such devices will function at the highest speed of today's surface ships while causing negligible drag.

Sonobuoys are the final type of local sonar. They consist of a hydrophone (underwater listening device) dropped into the water by ASW patrol planes or helicopters, and an antenna that remains on the surface to transmit acoustic data to the aircraft. Current models can lower a probe to as deep as 800 feet, to get below the thermal layers.

Escort sensors also include several nonacoustic devices. Besides radar, airborne ASW vehicles are also equipped with magnetic anomaly detectors to spot any variation in the earth's magnetic field such as that which the large iron mass of a submarine would cause. The entire oceanic magnetic field has been charted and the data stored in a computer. When comparison with the computerized chart indicates a variation, it is then matched with known magnetic properties of submarines (also stored in the computer's memory) for the final classification. Because of their short range, magnetic anomaly detectors are mainly used for final pinpointing and identification. There are indications, however, that advances are taking place in this type of sensing.

All the foregoing ASW systems are thoroughly integrated through an intricate network of ground-based, shipboard, and airborne computers. Sonic and radar signals can be compared with known "signatures" (tell-tale signs) of friendly and hostile submarines to identify them and predict their direction of travel. Reference systems between various sensors and arrays accurately locate a submarine, while television-type screens display all this information and electronic data-links inter-connect ASW bases, ships, and aircraft. The automation is profound.

Speaking of the strategic implications of ASW surveillance, DARPA Director Dr. George Heilmeier noted in 1976 that "if a majority of our submarines were to be kept under surveillance at all times, the vulnerability to preemptive attack would significantly reduce the deterrent effectiveness of our [submarine-based] ballistic missile forces."[63] Obviously, that logic applies in reverse to the Soviets; if we could track *all* of *their* missile submarines *all* of the time, they would cease to be a deterrent to a U.S. first strike. And since the United States is far ahead of the U.S.S.R. in ASW capabilities, it is really Moscow, not Washington, that must worry about the survival of its deterrent forces.

ASW Weapons

Cornering a modern nuclear-powered submarine is one thing but destroying it is another. Instruments for the kill, however, have not been neglected.

Torpedoes and depth charges spring readily to mind when talking about anti-submarine warfare. The Navy has torpedoes fired from aircraft and surface ships as well as from submarines. Submarines use the Mark-45 and Mark-48 torpedoes for ASW work. The Mark-45, also called ASTOR for anti-submarine torpedo, weighs 2,400 pounds and carries a nuclear warhead; the Mark-48 conventionally-armed torpedo weighs half again as much as ASTOR and is the principle ASW weapon carried by submarines. Aircraft and ships carry the Mark-46 ASW torpedo. Weighing only 580 pounds, it can dive 2,500 feet deep and travel twenty miles at speeds of over fifty miles an hour; if it misses the submarine on the first try it can turn around and attack again. An advanced lightweight torpedo (ALWT) is being developed to replace the Mark-46 in the late 1980s. It will be faster, have greater range and deeper search capabilities, and will carry a more powerful warhead.

Modern depth charges are far removed from the old "ash cans" that were thrown from World War II destroyers with Y-guns. The most common in use today are the Mark-57 and Mark-101 nuclear depth bombs dropped by ASW aircraft.

Mines are also receiving serious attention from the Navy. Two important models are CAPTOR and Quickstrike. CAPTOR (encapsulated torpedo) is a deep water mine which can be put in place by airplanes, ships, or submarines. It consists of a Mark-46 torpedo fit into a mine casing, along with acoustic sensors and a miniature computer which stores the sounds of submarines. As a submarine approaches, CAPTOR compares its sound with those stored in its memory, and, if it is an enemy, unleashes the Mark-46 torpedo. About a thousand CAPTORs are now waiting on ships and submarines around the world to be seeded into strategic areas when the need arises. Quickstrike is designed for shallower areas of the ocean and is now in production. There are also shallow water mines for harbors and bays that can be clandestinely ejected from a submarine torpedo tube and propel themselves to the desired location.

Completing the family of ASW weapons are the missiles. The oldest of these is ASROC (anti-submarine rocket) which is fired from ships. Weighing 1000 pounds, it consists of a Mark-46 torpedo or a nuclear depth-bomb attached to a rocket motor. The rocket separates when burned out and the bomb or torpedo continues on for about six miles. The counterpart to ASROC carried by submarines is SUBROC (submarine rocket) which weighs four tons and has a range of thirty miles. When a hostile submarine is detected, the missile is ejected from a torpedo tube and the rocket motor ignited. A nozzle steers the missile out of the water and toward the target at supersonic speed. After the motor separates a nuclear depth bomb coasts on to the target, sinks to an prescribed depth, and explodes.

ASW Platforms

The remaining components of the ASW suite are the platforms which carry the sensors and deploy the weapons. They can be classified as airborne, subsurface, and surface vehicles.

ASW aircraft operate from both land bases and ships. The Lockheed P-3 Orion is the current land-based plane. It can fly 2,000 miles, patrol for three hours, and return without refueling. Over 200 now take turns following Russia's missile-launching submarines around the world. They carry a full compliment of ASW sensors plus eight Mark-46 torpedoes and eight Mark-57 depth bombs. Orion is highly computerized: sensors, weapons, navigation instruments, and flight controls are all digitally interconnected. When a submarine is detected it is automatically pinpointed and classified. If the submarine is hostile the computer can select and launch the appropriate weapon while controlling a camera to photograph the results. Despite such sophistication, Navy officials are already designing a successor aircraft known as the VPX—VP being the Navy designation for land-based ASW squadrons. Reportedly designers are conceiving such exotic concepts as huge nuclear-powered aircraft that can stay aloft for weeks while sending out pilotless planes with sensors and weapons.

The Navy's principal carrier-based ASW aircraft is the Lockheed S-3A Viking, of which 187 are deployed. This twin-engined jet can remain on station without refueling for seven hours, and carries essentially the same sensors as Orion plus Mk-46 torpedoes, depth bombs, and mines. The Viking is even more highly automated than Orion. With an automatic landing system, it is just one step away from a pilotless ASW patrol craft. Most U.S. warships also carry ASW helicopters, which come equipped with sonobuoys, radar, magnetic anomaly detectors, and Mark-46 torpedoes.

Sophisticated V/STOL (vertical/short takeoff and landing) ASW aircraft are on the drawing boards. They will fly like a jet and hover like a helicopter to provide quick reaction and kill capacity against hostile subs. The first Navy V/STOL, the Type-A, will be a subsonic aircraft designed to replace the carrier-based Vikings in the 1980s. A follow-on supersonic Type-B will be operational in 1990, while a yet undefined Type-C is scheduled for deployment around the year 2000.

The hypothetical Soviet ASW threat cited by the Pentagon to justify such weapons as Trident is mostly conjecture or exaggeration; the evidence suggests that it is the United States that is rapidly acquiring the capacity to monitor every submarine in the ocean, thereby bringing us that much closer to a first-strike capability.

Subsurface ASW platforms include hunter-killer "attack" submarines, of which the Navy will eventually own 90. Attack subs use an intricate hull-mounted sonar combined with a towed array, but obviously do not need variable depth sonars because they are already below the thermal layers. Their armament includes torpedoes and SUBROC missiles, and they can also lay mines and place moored sensor buoys in position for area surveillance.

Surface ASW vessels are equipped with hull-mounted sonar, towed arrays, and variable depth sensors. About a hundred frigates, destroyers, and cruisers carry helicopters and can launch torpedoes and ASROC missiles (frigates only carry torpedoes). Thirteen aircraft carriers deploy ASW patrol planes plus helicopters. Many of these vessels are being modernized or replaced with new classes of warships such as the Spruance-class destroyers, nuclear-powered "strike cruisers," and some sort of helicopter or V/STOL-carrier.

The striking difference between U.S. and Soviet ASW capabilities is that the Russians tend to concentrate their tracking efforts close to their own waters and shipping lanes, rather than on ocean-wide surveillance. A report prepared by the Congressional Research Service of the Library of Congress states: "Today and in the near future the Soviets apparently have no effective open-ocean ASW, regardless of the scenario envisaged."[64]

Furthermore, Soviet technology is less advanced than America's. Besides having a strong advantage in satellite-borne sensor systems, the United States also enjoys significant leads in computers, integrated circuits, radars, surveillance instruments, and precision-guided weapons. According to Admiral R.Y. Kaufman, the United States has a predominant lead in ASW capabilities because it possesses a significant technological advantage in ASW sensors, ASW weapons, and submarine quieting.[65] Without more sophistication in these areas, the Soviets could not possibly locate and track many U.S. submarines.

The hypothetical Soviet ASW threat cited by the Pentagon to justify such weapons as Trident is mostly conjecture or exaggeration; the evidence suggests that it is the United States that is rapidly acquiring the capacity to monitor every submarine in the ocean, thereby bringing us that much closer to a first-strike capability. As pointed out by the Library of Congress report:

> . . . The United States engages in a wide range of ASW activities. Not only are the various components being upgraded, but they are being coherently and systematically integrated. Indeed it is the achievement of mutually reinforcing relationships among the individual elements, rather than the incremental improvements to particular programs, that accounts for the rapid overall increase in ASW effectiveness.[66]

The report further states:

> . . . If the United States achieves a disarming first-strike capability against Soviet ICBMs, and also develops an ASW capability that, together with attacks on naval facilities, could

practically negate the Soviet SSBN force, then the strategic balance as it has come to be broadly defined and accepted would no longer be stable.[67]

Then the report gives this cogent warning: "current trends in U.S. ASW programs should fall under close scrutiny."[68]

Ballistic Missile
and Bomber Defense

No matter how effectively a weapon performs, or how well a military operation is planned, experience suggests that something will go wrong. If U.S. officials were planning a disarming first strike against the U.S.S.R., the most obvious malfunction they would have to allow for would be the failure to completely destroy Soviet retaliatory weapons. To prevent damage to American cities, there would have to be some way to intercept that residual retaliation. This is where ballistic missile defense fits into the Pentagon's first-strike scenarios.

Like anti-submarine warfare, ballistic missile defense is divided into two categories: area and point. In essence, *area defense* means defending the entire United States against missile attack. *Point defense* simply means defending a certain geographic point, such as missile silos or radar sites. The United States was well on its way towards deployment of an anti-ballistic missile (ABM) system known as Safeguard, consisting of Spartan long-range missiles and Spring point-defense missiles, when the ABM Treaty was signed on May 26, 1972. The Treaty defines an ABM system as "a system to counter strategic missiles or their elements in flight trajectory." Such systems are composed of three components: interceptors, launchers, and radar.

Two ABM sites are allowed each country, but they must be confined to two 185-mile diamater circles at least 800 miles apart. One can be centered on the national capital and the other to defend an ICBM complex. Only 100 missile launchers are allowed at each site and they must be capable of firing only one interceptor with no quick reload capability. The treaty also bans systems or components which may be substituted for the existing hardware. This provision effectively prohibits deployment of futuristic concepts such as killer lasers or particle beam weapons as well as other-than-radar sensors which could be used for ballistic missile defense. Developing and testing of such systems, however, is not prohibited. Furthermore, development of air-based, space-based, sea-based, or mobile-land-based anti-missile systems is a violation of the ABM Treaty. A protocol to the ABM Treaty, signed in 1974 and ratified by both countries, reduces the number of ABM sites to one.

After the treaty was signed, the Pentagon immediately

dismantled its partly constructed second ABM site in Montana. Its Grand Forks, North Dakota site became operational in October 1974, but was ordered shut down by Congress in 1975.

Bomber Defense

In 1974, in recognition of the fact that maintenance of a bomber defense capability is basically pointless in the missile age, Air Force interceptor squadrons dwindled to twelve while the Army's elaborate network of Nike-Hercules anti-aircraft missiles was shut down. Two years later, then Defense Secretary Donald Rumsfeld reaffirmed that a major bomber defense—in the absence of a comparable anti-missile capability—would be a misuse of resources in an era of massive missile threats. By the end of 1976, however, the Air Force announced a new $2.5 billion program to modernize its anti-bomber system. In its FY 1978 budget proposal, it asked for a $30 million down payment on the purchase of 1970 new interceptor aircraft to replace the aging F-106 fighter. Obviously this move represents a significant shift from previous Pentagon doctrine.

Bomber warning systems are also being modernized. The distant early warning line (DEWLINE) of radars and the Joint Surveillance System radars are being automated. Existing radar surveillance aircraft are being replaced with the ultra-sophisticated AWACS (Airborne Warning And Control System) radar plane. Also, a new over-the-horizon radar is being installed to provide warning of enemy bombers and cruise missiles while they are still a thousand miles off our coast.

Radar, although the key to existing air defense warning systems, is susceptible to jamming and anti-radiation missiles. If bombers could be detected with a passive sensor (one which does not emit any radiation), there would be no danger of U.S. warning systems being knocked out in an enemy attack. Such a system is "Teal Ruby," DARPA's new multi-million dollar infra-red sensor which focuses on that part of the spectrum most prominent in jet exhaust gases. It is a mosaic array of about a quarter-million infrared detectors with integral silicon chip data-processing. Such chips are also used in pocket calculators and digital watches. Teal Ruby is the forerunner of a new system being developed to detect and track aircraft from space. A satellite containing such mosaic sensors will be put in orbit during one of the early space shuttle flights.

The increased activity in bomber and cruise missile defense raises questions about the direction of missile defense programs.

To assess these developments, warning systems are a more obvious index to military trends than the more secretive weapons world.

Missile Early Warning

U.S. missile warning systems now include the Ballistic Missile Early Warning System (BMEWS) and early warning satellites. BMEWS is a string of radars, now being upgraded, deployed in Alaska, Greenland, and the United Kingdom. Three early warning satellites watch for Soviet ICBM and SLBM launches. These satellites can only track missiles during their powered flight, however, because after the rocket motors burn out the infrared signal is not strong enough for existing sensors.

Other U.S. warning systems include the perimeter acquisition radar (PAR) from the Safeguard ABM system, which had been turned over to the Air Force for early warning use. PAR is a long-range radar that can track reentry bodies as well as missiles, and predict their targets. Also, two new "Pave Paws" phased-array radars will facilitate watching for SLBMs over the Atlantic and Pacific. Phased-array radar is a concept similar to mosaic infrared sensors, employing a stationary array of many detectors which together provide a composite picture of greater intensity.

Looking to the future, DARPA has a program called High Altitude Large Optics (HALO) which will employ mosaic sensors with integrated data-processing systems to provide day or night, all weather detection of hostile missiles. Its mosaic sensors contain as many as 100,000 detectors per square inch of surface with integral readout and processing circuitry. The whole system, with millions of detector cells, is positioned at the focal plane of an infrared telescope. The array of detectors, each looking at a different spot, act simultaneously to locate enemy missiles. HALO's long-wave infrared (LWIR) detectors can also track missiles during the final, coast phase by filtering out the background radiation produced by the earth, moon, and stars. In effect, LWIR sensors used in this manner violate the ABM Treaty by deploying a component to replace ABM radars and by putting that component in space. Nevertheless, HALO is envisioned as a replacement for current early warning satellites in the 1980s.

Homing Interceptor Technology

The ambitious activity in early warning programs raises suspicions that something must also be in the works to shoot those enemy missiles down. We cannot go into all aspects of the ballistic missile defense, but will concentrate on the two most significant systems. The first is Homing Interceptor Technology (HIT), a program shrouded in deep secrecy but about which some clues have appeared. HIT vehicles are described as miniature non-nuclear warheads that can be launched with existing booster rockets. The HIT warhead is less than a foot long, appears to be about seven inches in diameter, and weighs about 14 pounds. (The HIT warhead to be used against satellites is apparently larger.) A LWIR sensor guides it to the target and the hostile vehicle is destroyed by impact energy as the HIT warhead dispenses a cloud of metal pellets in its path. The pellets are fired in shotgun fashion and even if just one pellet collides at its closing speed of 27,000 miles per hour, the target would be finished.

Homing interceptor technology dates back to 1961, when the anti-satellite program Project Blackeye considered deployment of a screen of metal pellets along a hostile satellite's trajectory. Also, prior to 1969 the BAMBI (ballistic missile boost intercept) program considered the possibility of intercepting enemy missiles early in flight. If HIT vehicles were based close enough to the Soviet Union, they could conceivably be used to destroy Russian missiles before they started releasing MIRVs. Vought Corporation now has a contract from the Army Ballistic Missile Defense Command to develop a HIT warhead for use against missiles. Vought also has an Air Force contract to develop the anti-satellite HIT vehicle.

Ballistic missile defense hinges, of course, on access to extremely fast computer systems. Even the Illiac-4 is not adequate. For this reason, the Army is developing a super computer called the Parallel Element Processing Ensemble (PEPE) which will have between 300 and 900 minicomputers working in parallel and feeding into a master computer.

Directed Energy Weapons

The other significant anti-missile system is, if anything, more shrouded in secrecy than HIT. In 1976 the Army, as part of its missile defense work in an Advanced Technology Program, was "investigating revolutionary technologies—lasers, infrared sensors, (deleted)." But the censor forgot to erase the missing expression from an accompanying chart which revealed that the secret technology was "directed energy."[69] (In earlier years it was referred to by the sanitized title of "new concepts."[70])

"Directed energy" is the term used to describe such exotic

The first known laser beam was activated in 1960, and DARPA started investigating its potential military uses in 1962.... In 1975, demonstrations at the Naval Weapons Lab at China Lake, California showed that high-energy lasers could inflict structural damage on an aircraft. More recently, in 1978, a laser prototype was tested against much smaller and faster anti-tank missiles with reportedly high success.

weapons concepts as killer lasers and sub-atomic particle beams which reputedly can zap missiles out of the sky in a split second. The first known laser beam was activated in 1960, and DARPA started investigating its potential military uses in 1962. The discovery of chemical lasers in 1968 made high-energy (killer) lasers practical. In 1975, demonstrations at the Naval Weapons Lab at China Lake, California showed that high-energy lasers could inflict structural damage on an aircraft. More recently, in 1978, a laser prototype was tested against much smaller and faster anti-tank missiles with reportedly high success.

In 1975 DARPA reoriented its stepped-up laser program toward small, pulsing chemical lasers with ultra-precise aiming and tracking schemes for spacecraft use. Chemical lasers are particularly adapted for satellite deployment because they require no electrical energy, take advantage of the low temperatures to simplify cooling, and release the highly toxic by-products where they are unlikely to cause harm. In space, the unique properties of a laser—its ability to precisely concentrate energy at extreme distances with the speed of light—can be fully utilized. Preliminary studies indicated the United States could position an experimental laser gun in space by 1982.

Concentrated beams of sub-atomic charged particles, such as protons, are another form of directed energy which the United States has considered for missile defense since 1960. Particle beams have an advantage over high energy lasers in bad weather, and may have a longer range in the atmosphere if the problem of beam scattering can be overcome. Such beams are, however, affected by the earth's magnetic field which may make them less desirable for space-borne operations.

Today the Army is pursuing development of a neutral particle beam to be mounted on a space platform for destroying ballistic missiles in flight. Called *Sipapu* (an American Indian word for *sacred fire*), this neutrally charged beam would be unaffected by the earth's magnetic pull. The Air Force is also interested in *Sipapu* for anti-satellite work and a small space-based nuclear reactor is being developed to provide the necessary power. In addition, the very precise pointing system under development for astronomical satellites is finding weapons applications for aiming particle beams and lasers.

In spite of the Pentagon's long-standing and ambitious efforts in the area of directed energy weapons, there are still those who say the Russians are ahead in this field. Such charges have been rejected by the Carter administration, which suggests the United States leads in some aspects while the U.S.S.R. is ahead in others. But regardless of the apparent obstacles, some military experts believe that directed energy weapons, at least of the laser type (where the United States apparently has the technical advantage) will be a reality in a few years.

Only in the absence of the ABM Treaty's restrictions does all of this research activity make sense, since directed energy ABM weapons and mosaic sensors would constitute a violation. While Washington appears committed to that document, the Pentagon may be planning for its demise—and is readying the components of an air-tight first-strike capability.

Command, Control, and Communication

Command, Control, and Communication is abbreviated C-cubed or C^3. An effective first-strike capability requires that all of the many separate systems involved be integrated coherently. This coherence is made possible by an intricate system of command and control centers around the world and a communication network ranging from satellites to huge underground antenna grids; from extreme high to extreme low frequencies. A gargantuan intelligence operation bolstered by rapid—almost instantaneous—processing of data and computer automation supports these functions.

Command and Control

The worldwide military command and control system starts with the *war room* in the Pentagon which, in times of national emergency, falls under the control of the National Command Authority—the President and the Secretary of Defense. The war room has direct communication with all military information sources and has instantaneous access to massive computerized data files which display critical information on large television-type screens. But the war room is vulnerable and for that reason there are two alternate national command posts—one an underground duplication of the war room and the other airborne. The airborne national command post is a specially designed Boeing 747 and is considered the most survivable.

Major subordinate commands in Europe and the Pacific as well as the Strategic Air Command also have the same three types of command posts. Next down the line of command are the control centers, such as the underground launch control centers for silo-based missiles and their alternate airborne launch control centers which can take over if the primary ones are destroyed.

Redundancy is prominent in command and control and, at least ostensibly, should provide a survivable system. But only during an actual nuclear war can this performance be evaluated, and by then it will be too late.

Communication

An extensive global communication network keeps the command and control centers in constant touch with all military and intelligence operations. It ranges from common telephone lines to complicated satellite relay stations and spans the complete range of frequencies available. Every type of communication from ordinary voice to encrypted voice and rapid digital transmission of data is possible.

Extreme low frequency, very low frequency and low frequency are transmitted by massive antenna networks, some buried underground or trailing 5½ miles behind special aircraft, to communicate with submarines and possibly underground command posts. Medium to very high frequencies are used for the more conventional types of communication. High frequency is also used for over-the-horizon radar, very high frequency for conventional radar and televised data links, and ultra high or super high frequences for microwave radar as well as satellite communication and high speed data rates. Extreme high is used for communication with and between satellites.

Each of these frequencies and systems has advantages and disadvantages with respect to functioning in an atmosphere ionized by nuclear explosions, resistance to jamming, and surviving attack or sabotage. The best system is selected for a specific purpose, and redundancy is the rule.

A book could be written on military communication alone but this brief description is enough to convey the enormity of the network.

Intelligence Gathering

Intelligence gathering comprehends a range of activities from spies and listening posts in foreign lands to satellites. We have already discussed much of this aspect in other sections—sensors, missile and bomber warning, submarine tracking, space object identification, and the various satellite functions. Much of today's intelligence gathering is performed by satellites.

Data-gathering types of satellites can be broadly classed as *warning, meteorological,* and *reconnaissance* (spy). Warning satellites have already been discussed and, to a certain extent, so have meteorological spacecraft. Seasat and ocean surveillance satellites would best fit under the latter classification although they also perform a spy function. The true military weather satellites are of the *Block-5D* family, which are paired in polar, sub-synchronous orbits. That means one always takes cloud cover pictures at morning or evening and the other at noon or midnight.

Big Bird is the most famous of U.S. spy satellites. It is basically a 12-ton orbiting camera. Only one is in the sky at a time where it stays for four or five months in very low orbit. It transmits information to various land stations and sometimes drops a film capsule. Other types of spy satellites are search-and-find and electronic ferret; the latter pinpoints the source of various radio and radar signals. Civilian satellites such as Landsat also perform military intelligence missions.

Data Processing and Computerization

As with the various weapons systems it controls, computerized automation is crucial to C³. Illiac-4, PEPE, and silicon chip microprocessors in mosaic infrared sensors have been previously discussed.

The startling consequence of advanced information technology is that computers are now being programmed to make the decisions because the human being cannot keep up with the processing and handling of such a mass of data. One former defense official summed it up this way:

> ... *Computers are extremely important ... No human mind can enter the real time decision making loop and control the system. It has to be pre-programmed with logic so the computer can make the decision and run the game.*[71]

We could then justifiably ask who does have control, if anyone, when the computer is running the game. We have always relied on the Constitution-provided safeguard of civilian control over the military, but how does that work in today's automated nuclear age? A former Deputy Director of Defense Research and Engineering explained that:

> ... *It is no use to give [the President] a room full of status boards and say, "Here it is, boss, make a decision." It has to be boiled down to a scale—for example green, yellow or red—and he can decide by how far the needle moves, what he should do.*[72]

Now it really is getting scary. The true decision maker is the one who controls the movement of the needle. Who is well enough informed of the factual flux to choose the proper color? A former DARPA director contributed this insight:

. . . Human limitations in formulating and communicating commands will be a central difficulty in increasingly complex command, control and communication systems. In anticipating this problem, DARPA has initiated research aimed at developing and demonstrating a new type of command system cybernetics, principally concerned with the development of a new technology for information management.[73]

This new command system has also been referred to as *machine intelligence.* The goal of this research is to imbue computers with the ability to infer and deduce, as opposed to their traditional logic task of numerical processing.

When an international crisis arises, the computers will be humming and driving the needle from green to yellow to red. With both superpowers prepared only for second-strike retaliation—to deter the other from striking first—it is unlikely that either one would intentionally launch a nuclear weapon. But! . . . if the United States obtains a disarming first-strike capability, or even approaches it, we can be certain that in a crisis situation there will be nervous fingers poised over *the button.* The slightest miscalculation of the other's thoughts—or some extraneous computer inference—would provide the deadly twitch to slide aside the silo covers and raise the submarine launch tube hatches. A blink of the wrong light on the display panel will, in microseconds, signal the flash of nuclear cremation.

The Russian Threat

We have now seen a spectrum of Pentagon activity that indicates development of a knock-out first-strike capability against the Soviet Union. It has been my experience that this seemingly overwhelming indictment has a disturbing effect on people once they absorb it, but almost invariably produces the question: "What about the Russians?" That is what we will address now.

It is the alleged Russian threat that has enlisted so many legislators and taxpayers to support weapons programs. Yet the most readily available information concerning that threat comes from the very source that wants the arms: the Pentagon hierarchy. They are set up as the authority, but what data they do release is either slanted and fractured, or is buried in such a deluge of irrelevant material that the key facts remain isolated. It takes some research and a little experience with military-industrial thinking to separate knowledge from nonsense. A good place to start is a brief excursion into history, because it has much to tell us about the arms race.

History of the Arms Race

The nuclear age was kicked off with Albert Einstein's letter to President Roosevelt in 1939 suggesting the possibility of producing an atomic bomb. On December 2, 1942, the first chain reaction was achieved at the University of Chicago. Four years later (and over a year after the first U.S. atomic explosion), the Soviets also achieved a chain reaction. Likewise, it was four years after the bombing of Hiroshima and Nagasaki that the Russians detonated their first A-bomb. On August 24, 1949, the day after the Soviet's first nuclear test, the North Atlantic Treaty Organization (NATO) came into existence. Almost six years elapsed before the Warsaw Pact was signed. In 1954 the U.S. deployed "tactical" nuclear weapons in Europe, a move which was duplicated three years later by the Soviets. These are examples of what has been called the "action-reaction cycle" of the arms race—an initiative by the United States, a reaction by the U.S.S.R.

In the early 1950s, the American public heard frightening stories about a vastly superior Russian bomber force. The so-called "bomber gap" was invented to justify deployment of the

Pentagon's B-52 fleet. Later the gap turned out to be a myth, but its purpose had already been served. In fact, the U.S.S.R. had felt so hopelessly outclassed in the bomber age that it tried to jump precipitously into the missile age. On August 26, 1957, the Soviets announced their first ICBM flight, and that was followed in a couple months by putting Sputnik in orbit. President Eisenhower responded immediately by setting up the Gaither Committee to investigate the Soviet missile threat and authorized U-2 flights over the U.S.S.R. to help determine its capabilities. Gaither Committee findings showed that by 1959 the Soviets could launch 100 ICBMs against the United States, thus creating the missile gap.

History has proved that the missile gap was just as fictitious as the bomber gap. Rather than building a huge ICBM force, the Soviets were concentrating their efforts on shorter-range missiles for use in Europe. The ICBM and Sputnik launches were more showcase demonstrations than full-scale production programs. As shown in the top portion of Figure 6, in 1960 the Soviets had only 35 ICBMs, compared to 18 for the U.S. That temporary 17-missile lead was the famous missile gap. Nevertheless, it served to accelerate production of U.S. ICBMs as well as SLBMs, as Figure 6 indicates. The U.S.S.R. responded to the U.S. buildup several years later, and the arms race reached new momentum.

In 1960 the first Polaris ballistic missile submarine was launched. Five years later, the Soviet Union put its first comparable ballistic missile submarine to sea. The Soviets had in 1960 launched their first diesel-powered Golf-class missile submarine, which carried three SS-N-4 ballistic missiles of 350 nautical miles (n.m.) range, but that could hardly be classed as a strategic weapon. It was not until 1968, however, with the launch of their first Yankee-class boat equipped with sixteen 1,300 n.m. SS-N-6 missiles that the Soviets had anything comparable to Polaris subs with 1,200 n.m. Polaris A-1 missiles. By that time, of course, the United States had already discarded the A-1 and the follow-on A-2, and had deployed the 2,500 n.m. Polaris A-3 with its triple-header MRVs. By then, moreover, the MIRVed Poseidon was being flight-tested. The bottom portion of Figure 6 shows the SLBM comparison.

Turning to MIRVs, we find that the Soviets first tested them in 1973—five years after the first U.S. tests. MIRVs were first deployed by the United States in 1970 and by the U.S.S.R. in 1975. Current U.S. weapons programs—such as maneuverable warheads and strategic cruise missiles—can be expected to elicit similar efforts from the Soviet Union in a few years. Ironically, it is that predictable response that is used to justify *current*

67

Pentagon procurement drives.

As Figure 6 suggests, the Soviet Union caught up with and exceeded the United States in numbers of ICBMs and SLBMs around 1970. The Pentagon's switch from quantity to quality during the latter half of the last decade underlies U.S. adherence to the 1972 SALT-I agreements.

SALT-I and Equivalence

Most experts generally agree that when the SALT-I accords were signed there was a rough degree of equivalence between U.S. and Soviet strategic capabilities. In effect, the Interim Agreement on Offensive Weapons merely froze the planned inventory for each country. Figure 7 depicts the numbers of arms allowed each side under SALT-I.

Despite complaints by some cold war advocates that the United States was sold short on that temporary five-year agreement, there are definite reasons why the Soviets were allowed greater numbers. Some of them are:

1) The U.S. deployment of MIRVs contributed to America's three-fold advantage in deliverable warheads.

2) Intercontinental bombers were not covered by the Interim Agreement, and the United States had 350-450 compared to only 140 for the Soviets. (The exact number in the Strategic Air Command is questionable because Pentagon figures of bomber losses in Vietnam are much lower than Hanoi's.)

3) The U.S. had "tactical" nuclear weapons and forward-based bombers in Europe which could reach the Soviet homeland.

4) America's NATO allies (Britain and France) also have nuclear-armed missiles and missile-launching submarines.

5) The Pentagon's forward bases in Scotland, Spain, and Guam allow America's ballistic missile submarines to stay "on station" up to 50 percent longer than Russia's.

6) Other characteristics of weapons and submarines (readiness, reliability, accuracy) favor the United States.

So, in effect, all the SALT-I Agreement does is allow the Soviets to offset in numbers what they lack in quality. It did not, however, freeze quality improvements—the area of greatest U.S. emphasis.

Comparison of Weapons

In many areas the United States outshines the Soviet Union in weapons sophistication. However, two new Soviet weapons receiving a lot of publicity in the United States are being used to justify new U.S. weapons programs. They are the SS-18 missile and the Delta submarine. The SS-18 is an ICBM that is replacing the huge SS-9 missile. It has a 7,000 n.m. range and can carry ten warheads of two-megaton yield each. These are the awesome characteristics we read about in Pentagon statements. What we do not hear about is the fact that the SS-18 will have an accuracy of only about 1,500 feet, which is not as good as the 1,200-foot CEP of existing Minuteman-3 missiles *before* accuracy improvement. With the NS-20 guidance package and Mark-12A warheads, Minuteman-3 will have the same chance of destroying three silos as an SS-18 (54.7 percent chance for Minuteman and 54.3 for the SS-18). That means that only 300 of the U.S.'s 550 Minuteman-3 missiles are as potent as the entire SS-18 force allowed by SALT-II.

I must reluctantly conclude from the evidence that the United States is ahead now and is rapidly approaching a first-strike capability—which it should start deploying by the mid-1980s. The Soviet Union, meanwhile, seems to be struggling for a second best. There is no available evidence that the U.S.S.R. has the combined missile lethality, anti-submarine warfare potential, ballistic missile defense, or space warfare technology to attain a disabling first-strike before the end of this century, if then.

In addition to hard target kill potential, the basing distribution of strategic weapons is critical to their ultimate effectiveness. At least three-quarters of all Soviet strategic warheads are carried on silo-based ICBMs which are becoming more vulnerable to U.S. missiles. Only one-quarter of U.S. warheads are so based. Moreover, 60 percent of all American warheads are in submarines which cannot be destroyed by any of the ICBMs or SLBMs the Soviets are developing or have deployed.[76]

Delta submarines have frequently been used to justify the new Trident weapons system. Actually, the only area of comparison is that the Delta's SS-N-8 SLBM has a 4,200 n.m. range—about the same as the Trident-1 missile. The similarity ends there. The first thirteen Delta (Delta-1) subs had twelve launch tubes. In 1976 a

Figure 6
ICBM and SLBM Buildup[74]

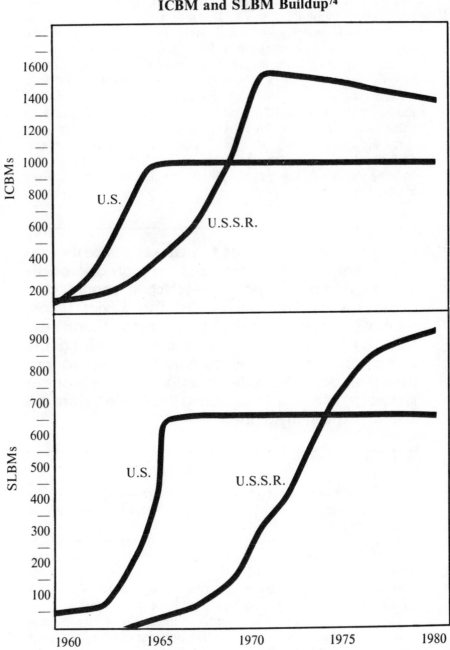

Figure 7
Strategic Weapons Allowed by SALT-I[75]

	U.S.	U.S.S.R.
ICBMs	1,054	1,618
SLBMs	656*	740**
Ballistic Missile Submarines	41*	62

*If the 54 U.S. Titan-2 ICBMs are dismantled, these figures could be raised to 710 SLBMs in 44 submarines.

**If the 210 SS-7 and SS-8 ICBMs are dismantled, this figure could be raised to 950 SLBMs.

"stretch" version (the Delta-2) was launched with sixteen missiles—the same number as Polaris and Poseidon subs, while the new Trident ship will have 24 missile launch tubes.

The SS-N-8 SLBM has a single warhead with an accuracy of about 4,800 feet and a 1.56 lethality rating. Existing Poseidon warheads are almost as potent (K = 1.3 per RV) and there are *over thirteen times as many* on each submarine. Indeed, Poseidon submarines are over eleven times as lethal as Delta-2s. The new 100-kiloton Trident-1 warhead, however, with its 1,500-foot CEP will have a lethality of 3.34—over twice that of the SS-N-8—and there will be *twelve to sixteen times as many on each Trident sub.*

The Soviets have a follow-on SLBM for the 16-tube Delta subs which is designated SS-N-18 and has three MIRVs. That means Delta-2 submarines will have 48 reentry bodies each. The SS-N-18 MIRVs have a lethality of 1.37—less than the SS-N-8 and about the same as each Poseidon warhead. This Soviet capability is vastly inferior to the 408 target-homing MARVs that could be carried on each Trident submarine when Trident-2 missiles are deployed—each warhead having the maximum lethality possible.

This bring us to the question of whether the Soviet Union has a counterforce capability. Since counterforce is a matter of degree we must say that they do. That is largely academic however. The real question is who has the *most* counterforce capability now and who is adding more the fastest, for the ultimate goal of counterforce improvements is the ability to inflict an unanswerable first-strike. I must reluctantly conclude from the evidence that the United States is ahead now and is rapidly approaching a first-strike capability—which it should start deploying by the mid-1980s. The Soviet Union, meanwhile, seems to be struggling for a second best. There is no available evidence that the U.S.S.R. has the combined missile lethality, anti-submarine warfare potential, ballistic missile defense, or space warfare technology to attain a disabling first-strike before the end of this century, if then.

Epilogue

In this document, I have given a brief view of the evidence which suggests that the United States is moving toward a knock-out first-strike. I do not mean to imply that everyone in government or the Pentagon is conspiring to destroy Russia. There may be some who would like to see that happen and possibly others who just seek more nuclear leverage for diplomatic advantage. Most Americans, I feel, are sincere in their desire for peace but are caught up in the momentum of the arms race and fear the implied consequences if the status quo is abandoned.

Complicating the situation, however, is the drive for profits by large weapons producers. Military prime contracting now exceeds $42 billion annually, and the return on equity is high—in some cases between twenty and fifty percent.[77] Large corporations have hundreds of offices within walking distance of the Capitol building from which they conduct constant lobbying. Even the Pentagon appears controlled by the corporate arm of the military-industrial complex. Admiral Hyman G. Rickover says "the great difficulty in conducting defense business is that most of the top officials come from industry. They naturally have an industry viewpoint . . . "[78]

On the other hand, these same weapons contractors turn their hats around when business opportunities appear in other areas. For instance, Lockheed and Boeing, two of America's leading arms builders, sought export licenses to sell their jetliners to the Soviet Union. The Bank of America, which has many ties to the aerospace industry, has a representative office in Moscow and its vice president has advocated increased trade with the Soviets, arguing that there is no risk in dealing with them because they have always lived up to their commercial agreements.[79] The pattern seems to be that the Soviet threat surges when there is a need to drum up support for weapons contracts, but shrinks as opportunities to market U.S. goods in Russia present themselves.

Fear of losing jobs is another obstacle to disarmament. Many legislators are trapped in that dilemma: wanting on the one hand to use some military funds to meet human and social needs while, on the other, fearful of losing jobs of constituents back home. An analysis of the employment data suggests, however, that weapons programs are very inefficient at providing employment. The Trident-1 missile is an example. Information from Lockheed public relations indicates that 8,000 people will work on Trident-

73

1 during its peak—about half at Lockheed's missile plant in Santa Clara County, California, and the remainder for subcontractors. In FY 1977 Lockheed received a $1.1 billion contract to manufacture 80 missiles. Based on Santa Clara County's 160,000 manufacturing jobs which were expected to turn out $9 billion worth of goods during that year, Trident amounts to twelve percent of the manufacturing output while only employing five percent of that work force.

I have brought up these subjects because I realize they are very real concerns to many people. I have experienced them myself. Nevertheless, if we are going to achieve a more meaningful life for ourselves and a just distribution of the earth's resources for every person, we will have to dispel the Pentagon's deceptions. The counterforce gap and the military-spending gap that we are told exist today are no more real than the bomber gap or the missile gap of past years.

It is my observation that only a small portion of the people who even recognize this lethal momentum are motivated to do anything about it. Yet the risks to personal freedom and security those few are taking are minute compared to the risk of nuclear cremation which faces us all if the arms race continues to its ultimate conclusion. Those few people may well be the single remaining hope for civilization. The importance of their efforts cannot be overstated.

Notes

1. *The Fiscal Year 1968-72 Defense Program and 1968 Defense Budget,* statement of Secretary of Defense Robert McNamara before a joint session of the Senate Armed Services Committee and the Senate Subcommittee on Department of Defense Appropriations (January 23, 1967), p. 39.

2. Jarvenpaa, Pauli; *Flexible Nuclear Options: New Myths and Old Realities,* Cornell University Peace Studies Program Occasional Paper Number 7 (September 1976), p. 48.

3. *Counterforce Issues for the US Strategic Nuclear Forces,* Congressional Budget Office Background Paper (January 1978), p. 32.

4. *Foreign Affairs* (January 1956), pp. 187-189.

5. *Annual Defense Department Report FY 1975,* By Secretary of Defense James R. Schlesinger (1974), Part 2, p. 33.

6. Commencement address of Secretary of Defense Robert McNamara at Ann Arbor, Michigan on June 16, 1962. Reprinted in *The Department of State Bulletin,* XLVII (July 9, 1962), pp. 64-69.

7. For a fuller discussion of the history of proposed legislation to improve missile accuracy see Ball, Desmond J.; "The Counterforce Potential of American SLBM Systems," *Journal of Peace Research* (International Peace Research Institute, Oslo, Norway; Vol. XIV, No. 1, 1977), pp. 31-32.

8. *US Foreign Policy for the 1970s: A New Strategy for Peace,* a report to Congress by President Richard M. Nixon (February 18, 1970), p. 122.

9. Leitenberg, Milton; "The Race to Oblivion," *Bulletin of the Atomic Scientists* (September 1974), p. 9.

10. See UPI dispatch "Nuclear Policy Switch: New Accuracy, Power Sought for Warheads," *San Jose Mercury* (August 10, 1972), p. 1.

11. Ibid.

12. Foreign policy address to Congress by President Richard M. Nixon (May 1973).

13. Address by Secretary of Defense James R. Schlesinger at the Overseas Writers Association Luncheon in Washington, D.C. on January 10, 1974. Excerpts reprinted in "Flexible Strategic Options and Deterrence," *Survival* (Vol. XVI, No. 2, March/April 1974), pp. 86-90.

14. *Fiscal Year 1975 Authorization for Military Procurement, Research and Development, and Active Duty, Selected Reserve and Civilian Personnel Strengths,* hearings before the Senate Armed Services Committee (February 5, 1974), Part 1, p. 265.

15. UPI dispatch "US Favors First Use of N-Weapons," *San Jose Mercury* (May 31, 1975).

16. *Department of Defense Annual Report Fiscal Year 1979,* by Secretary of Defense Harold Brown (February 2, 1978), p. 53.

17. This number does not include B-52 bombers which are mothballed or have been transferred to other missions such as ocean surveillance and mine laying.

18. At the time of this writing, at least one of the Poseidon submarines—the Francis Scott Key—has been converted to launch Trident-1 missiles and is scheduled to go to sea on its first strategic mission in October 1979.

19. Sources: *Aviation Week & Space Technology* (April 18, 1977), pp. 18-19 (Library of Congress Tables); *World Armament and Disarmament: SIPRI Yearbook 1977* (Stockholm, Sweden), p. 4; *Department of Defense Appropriations,* hearings before the House Appropriations Committee (September 20, 1977), Appendix to Part 7, p. 168; *Counterforce Issues for the US Strategic Nuclear Forces,* op cit., pp. 16-19; *Retaliatory Issues for the US Strategic Nuclear Forces,* Congressional Budget Office Background Paper (June 1978), pp. 6-9; *Aviation Week & Space Technology* (March 12, 1979), pp. 88-99; *Air Force Magazine* (March 1979), p. 23; *The Military Balance 1976/77, 1977/78, 1978/79,* (International Institute for Strategic Studies, London, England); *Aviation Week & Space Technology* (October 31, 1977), pp. 46-47; *Aviation Week & Space Technology* (November 3, 1975), pp. 34-38; *Aviation Week & Space Technology* (October 13, 1975), pp. 15-19; *Aviation Week & Space Technology* (June 25, 1979), pp. 21-22. Mid-1979 quantitites estimated from trend in these sources.

20. Ibid, plus: *Sea Power* (May 1977), p. 30; *Air Force Magazine* (March 1979), pp. 99-101 and 111-112; *Hearings on Military Posture and HR 10929,* before the House Armed Services Committee (January 27, 1978), Part 7, p. 82.

21. Source: *The Defense Monitor* (Center for Defense Information, 122 Maryland Ave., NE, Washington, D.C.; Volume VIII, No. 2, February 1979), p. 4.

22. *Annual Defense Department Report FY 1978,* by Secretary of Defense Donald H. Rumsfeld (January 17, 1977), pp. 76-77.

23. *Aviation Week & Space Technology* (June 25, 1979), p. 23.

24. *Watsonville Register-Pajaronian* (November 5, 1977), "News in Brief."

25. For a more complete discussion of the measures of strategic power see Schneider, Barry R. and Leader, Stefan; "The United States-Soviet Arms Race, SALT, and Nuclear Proliferation," published in the *Congressional Record* (Senate; Vol. 121, No. 87; June 5, 1975).

26. Speech at the University of California at Los Angeles (UCLA), Westwood, Calif. (January 29, 1975). Cited in Schneider and Leader, op cit.

27. Cited in Schneider and Leader, op cit.

28. *United States Military Posture for FY 1979,* by Chairman of the Joint Chiefs of Staff General George S. Brown (January 20, 1978), p. 28.

29. *Aviation Week & Space Technology* (June 25, 1979), p. 22.

30. Schneider and Leader, op cit.

31. Source for equations to determine K and P_k: *Offensive Missiles: Stockholm Paper 5,* (Stockholm International Peace Research Institute, Stockholm, Sweden; 1974), pp. 16 and 18.

32. For a thorough discussion of K_{max} due to the cratering effect of nuclear weapons see: Tsipis, Kosta: *Nuclear Explosion Effects on Missile Silos* (Center for International Studies, Massachusetts Institute of Technology; February 1978), pp. 83-87.

33. *Offensive Missiles,* op cit.

34. UPI dispatch in *San Jose Mercury* (January 20, 1974).

35. Fiscal year 1975 authorization hearings before the Senate Armed Services Committee, op cit, (April 23, 1974), Part 7, p. 3766.

36. *Hearings on Military Posture and HR 11500* before the House Armed Services Committee (February 18, 1976), Part 5, p. 78.

37. *United States Military Posture for FY 1978,* op cit, p. 24.

38. *Fiscal Year 1977 Authorizations for Military Procurement, Research and Development, and Active Duty, Selected Reserves and Civilian Personnel Strengths,* hearings before the Senate Armed Services Committee (March 19, 1976), Part II, p. 6268.

39. Fiscal year 1975 authorization hearings before the Senate Armed Services Committee, op cit, (February 5, 1974), Part 1, p. 65.

40. *United States Military Posture for FY 1978,* op cit, p. 12.

41. Fiscal year 1975 authorization hearings before the Senate Armed Services Committee, op cit. (April 2, 1974), Part 6, pp. 3399-3400.

42. *Aviation Week & Space Technology* (May 10, 1976), p. 28.

43. *Aviation Week & Space Technology* (February 23, 1976), pp. 56-57.

44. *Hearings on Military Posture and HR 3689,* before the House Armed Services Committee (March 10, 1975), Part 3, p. 3443.

45. *Hearings on Military Posture and HR 11500,* op cit. (February 18, 1976), Part 4, p. 57.

46. *Hearings on Military Posture and HR 5068,* before the House Armed Services Committee (February 8, 1977), Part 4, p. 186.

47. Ibid, p. 184.

48. For a fuller discussion of Trident missile failures see Aldridge, Robert C.; "The Trident Fiasco: Obstacles on the Way to Doomsday," *The Nation* (August 16, 1975), pp. 115-116.

49. *Fiscal Year 1980 Arms Control Impact Statements* (March 1979), pp. 54-55.

50. *Annual Defense Department Report FY 1978,* op cit, p. 122.

51. Interim Agreement Unilateral Statement B on land-mobile ICBM launchers (May 26, 1972). See *SALT: The Moscow Agreements and Beyond,* edited by Mason Willrich and John B. Rhinelander (New York: The Free Press, 1974), p. 306.

52. *World Armaments and Disarmament: SIPRI Yearbook 1977,* op cit, p. 5.

53. McCartney, James; "President Pushes New Missiles Despite Arms Control Desires," *San Jose Mercury* (October 7, 1977), p. 9.

54. *Fiscal Year 1980 Arms Control Impact Statements,* op cit, pp. 24-25.

55. *Fiscal Year 1979 Arms Control Impact Statements* (June 1978), p. 21.

56. AP dispatch, "Hydrogen Aircraft Study Funded," *San Jose Mercury* (November 7, 1977), p. 8. Also see *Aviation Week & Space Technology* (November 14, 1977), p. 54.

57. *Department of Defense Authorization for Appropriations for Fiscal Year 1979,* hearings before the Senate Armed Services Committee (February 21, 1978), Part 2, p. 1109.

58. Silber, Howard; "Pentagon Study Aims at Bomber Advances," *Omaha World Herald* (May 28, 1978), p. 1.

59. *Aviation Week & Space Technology* (April 17, 1978), p. 31; and (September

11, 1978), pp. 109-112.

60. *Aviation Week & Space Technology* (November 8, 1976), p. 13.

61. Estimated from trend in *The Military Balance 1976/77, 1977/78, 1978/79,* op cit.

62. See Hussain, Farooq: "No Place to Hide," *New Scientist* (August 15, 1974).

63. *Defense Advanced Research Projects Agency Fiscal Year 1977 Research and Development Program Statement,* by George H. Heilmeier, Director (February 1976), pp. II-12.

64. *Evaluation of Fiscal Year 1979 Arms Control Impact Statements: Toward More Informed Congressional Participation in National Security Policymaking,* a report prepared for the House International Relations Committee by the Foreign Affairs and National Defense Division of the Congressional Research Service of the Library of Congress (January 3, 1979), p. 104.

65. Ibid, p. 107.

66. Ibid, p. 112.

67. Ibid, p. 119.

68. Ibid.

69. Fiscal year 1977 authorization hearings before the Senate Armed Services Committee, op cit. (March 30, 1976), Part 12, pp. 6704-6705.

70. *Fiscal Year 1976 and July-September 1976 Transition Period Authorization for Military Procurement, Research and Development, and Active Duty, Selected Reserve and Civilian Personnel Strengths,* hearings before the Senate Armed Services Committee (March 19, 1975), Part 6, p. 3252.

71. *Fiscal Year 1974 Authorization for Military Procurement, Research and Development, Construction Authorization of the Safeguard ABM, and Active Duty and Selected Reserve Strengths,* hearings before the Senate Armed Services Committee (February 21, 1973), Part 4, pp. 2210-2211.

72. *Hearings on Military Posture and HR 11500,* op cit. (February 20, 1976), Part 5, p. 230.

73. *DARPA Fiscal Year 1978 Program for Research and Development,* a statement by Dr. George H. Heilmeier, Director (February 1977), p. II-57.

74. Sources: *World Armaments and Disarmament: SIPRI Yearbook 1977,* op cit, pp. 24-25; *United States Military Posture for FY 1977,* by Chairman of the Joint Chiefs of Staff General George S. Brown (January 20, 1976), pp. 37-38; *SALT: The Moscow Agreements and Beyond,* op cit, p. 52; and fiscal year 1975 authorization hearings before the Senate, op cit, Part 7, p. 3865.

75. *Britannica Book of the Year 1973,* op cit, pp. 212-213

76. "Zeroing In On the Silo Busters," *Time* (May 9, 1977), p. 18.

77. See *Forbes* (January 1, 1977), p. 133; (January 9, 1978), p. 61; (January 8, 1979), p. 248.

78. *Defense Procurement in Relationships Between Government and Its Contractors,* hearings before a subcommittee of the House-Senate Joint Economic Committee (April 2, 1975), p. 2.

79. Hawkins, Ben; "Banker Urges Soviet Trade," *San Jose Mercury* (May 6, 1975).

Glossary

ABM — Anti-ballistic missile.

ABM Treaty — One of the SALT-I documents which limits defensive ABM interceptor missiles.

ABRES — Advanced Ballistic Reentry Systems.

Advanced Development — The phase of development following concept definition and preceding engineering development.

AFSATCOM — Air Force Satellite Communications System.

ALCM — Air-launched cruise missile.

ALWT — Advanced lightweight torpedo, planned successor for the Mark-46.

AMARV — Advanced maneuvering reentry vehicle.

Apollo — A U.S. space program administered by the National Aeronautics and Space Administration.

ASALM — Advanced strategic air-launched missile.

ASBM — Air-to-Surface Ballistic Missile.

ASROC — Anti-submarine rocket fired from surface ships.

ASTOR — Anti-submarine torpedo, the Mark-45 nuclear torpedo, fired from submarines.

ASW — Anti-submarine warfare.

Atlas — An early U.S. missile still being used as a test booster.

AWACS — Airborne Warning and Control System.

BAMBI — Ballistic Missile Booster Intercept, a program of the 1960s.

BMEWS — Ballistic Missile Early Warning System.

Burner-2 — An upper stage used with Thor missiles for precise maneuvering and positioning in space.

Bus — That portion of the missile which releases the multiple individually-targeted reentry vehicles (MIRVs). The formal name is Post-Boost Control System (PBCS).

BX — A heavy bomber of the future intended to overcome Soviet air defenses in the 1990s.

C³ — Command, control and communication (C-cubed).

CAPTOR — Encapsulated torpedo, a deep water anti-submarine mine.

Counterforce — A nuclear strategy whereby attack missiles are targeted against the opponent's military emplacements.

Damage limitation — A strategic nuclear doctrine intended to limit damage to American cities by destroying Soviet nuclear weapons before they are launched.

DARPA — Defense Advanced Research Projects Agency.

Delta-1 submarine — A Soviet nuclear-powered ballistic missile submarine which carries twelve SS-N-8 missiles.

Delta-2 submarine — A stretched version of the Soviet's Delta-1 which carries sixteen SS-N-8 missiles.

Deterrence — A nuclear strategy whereby a potential aggressor is deterred from using nuclear weapons under threat of unacceptable retaliation.

DEWLINE — Distant early warning line of radars for bomber warning.

Directed energy — A term used to describe new weapons innovations such as killer lasers and charged particle beams.

DSCS — Defense Satellite Communications System.

ELF — Extreme low frequency.

Engineering development — All work necessary including testing which leads to a production decision.

Evader — A name given to the Mark-500 maneuvering reentry vehicle for Trident to imply its function is only to evade enemy interceptor vehicles.

FB-111A — Existing U.S. fighter-bombers.

FB-111H — A proposed stretch version of the FB-111A which would fill a requirement for a penetrating medium bomber.

FLTSATCOM — Fleet Satellite Communications System.

Fratricide — The effect of a nuclear explosion environment on other incoming warheads.

Galosh — A Soviet anti-ballistic missile interceptor, sixty-four of which are stationed around Moscow.

GEODSS — Ground-electro-optical deep space surveillance.

Geosynchronous orbit — A satellite orbit around the earth equator that takes twenty-four hours for one revolution; thus it stays at one point over the earth at the equater. Altitude for this type orbit is approximately 22,000 miles.

GLCM — Ground-launched cruise missile.

Golf class submarine — A Soviet diesel-powered ballistic missile submarine first deployed in 1960. It carries three SS-N-4 or SS-N-5 missiles.

HALO — High altitude large optics. A future satellite-based sensor for detecting and tracking ballistic missiles.

HIT — Homing interceptor technology. A nonnuclear interceptor for ballistic missiles and submarines.

Hotel class submarine — An early Soviet nuclear-powered ballistic missile submarine first deployed in 1964. It carries three SS-N-5 missiles.

ICBM — Intercontinental ballistic missile.

Illiac-4 — A powerful computer developed to process anti-submarine warfare surveillance data for the U.S. Navy. It is located at Moffett Naval Air Base in California.

Interim Agreement — One of the SALT-I documents. A temporary 5-year agreement to limit strategic weapons.

Kiloton — The nuclear explosive force equal to one-thousand tons of conventional high explosives.

Landsat — The U.S. earth resources satellite series.

Laser — A highly concentrated beam of light. Acronym for light amplification by stimulated emission of radiation.

Lethality — A number, expressed as "K," denoting the ability of a missile to destroy hard targets. The higher the number, the more lethal the weapon.

LWIR — Long wavelength infrared.

Mach — Mach numbers are used to denote the speed of a body relative to the speed of sound in the surrounding atmosphere; mach-1 being the speed of sound.

MAD — Mutual assured destruction.

Mark-12 reentry vehicle — The MIRV originally deployed on Minuteman-3 ICBMs.

Mark-12A reentry vehicle — A new warhead designed to replace Mark-12s on Minuteman-3 and possibly for use on Missile-X and Trident-2 missiles.

Mark-45 torpedo — A nuclear anti-submarine torpedo launched from submarines. Also called ASTOR.

Mark-46 torpedo — A lightweight anti-submarine torpedo launched from aircraft and submarines.

Mark-48 torpedo — The latest anti-submarine torpedo launched from submarines.

Mark-57 depth bomb — A nuclear depth bomb carried by anti-submarine patrol aircraft.

Mark-101 depth bomb — A nuclear depth bomb carried by anti-submarine patrol aircraft.

Mark-500 reentry vehicle — A maneuvering reentry vehicle (MARV) being developed for use on the Trident-1 missile.

MARV — Maneuvering reentry vehicle.

Megaton — The nuclear explosive force equal to one-million tons of conventional explosives.

Minuteman — A U.S. intercontinental ballistic missile. Currently deployed are the Minuteman-2 and Minuteman-3.

MIRV — Multiple individually-targeted reentry vehicle.

Missile-X — A new mobile intercontinental ballistic missile which the U.S. is developing. Sometimes referred to as M-X.

MRV — Multiple reentry vehicle but not individually targeted.

MSR — Missile site radar, once used at the Safeguard ABM site in North Dakota.

NASA — National Aeronautics and Space Administration.

NATO — North Atlantic Treaty Organization.

Nautical Mile — 1.15 statute miles or 1.85 kilometers.

Navstar — A global positioning system of 24 satellites being developed by the United States for 3-dimensional navigation and velocity.

NCA — National Command Authority.

NORAD — North American Air Defense Command.

NOSS — Naval ocean surveillance satellite.

ORICS — Optical Ranging, Identification and Communication System. A laser system being developed by the U.S. for detecting and communicating with submarines.

Orion — A U.S. land-based anti-submarine warfare airplane. Also designated P-3.

OTH — Over-the-horizon radar.

P-3 — The Orion land-based anti-submarine warfare aircraft of the U.S.

PAR — Perimeter acquisition radar. Formerly part of the Safeguard ABM system but now assigned to NORAD for missile early warning service.

Pave Paws — Two new U.S. phased array radars for detecting submarine launched ballistic missile launches in the Pacific and Atlantic. One is at Otis Air Force Base in Massachusetts and the other at Beale Air Force Base in California.

Payload — see "throw weight."

PEPE — Parallel element procesing ensemble. A high capacity computer being developed by the U.S. for ballistic missile defense.

PGRV — Precision guided reentry vehicle, a precision maneuvering reentry vehicle in development by the U.S.

P_k — Probability of kill.

Polar orbit — An orbit where the satellite's path goes over the North and South Poles.

Polaris — The United States' first nuclear-powered ballistic missile submarine. Also the first U.S. submarine-launched ballistic missiles of which there were three generations: the A-1, A-2, and A-3.

Poseidon — A U.S. ballistic missile launching submarine converted from Polaris boats. Also the Poseidon submarine-launched ballistic missile, successor to the Polaris A-3.

Quickstrike — A shallow water bottom mine.

S-2 aircraft — An older carrier-based anti-submarine warfare aircraft. Also called Tracker. Being replaced by the U.S. S-3A Viking.

S-3A — The United States' newest carrier-based anti-submarine warfare aircraft.

SAC — Strategic Air Command.

Safeguard — The single U.S. anti-ballistic missile base in North Dakota, now deactivated.

SAINT — Satellite Interceptor. A U.S. anti-satellite program of the 1960s.

SALT — Strategic Arms Limitations Talks between the U.S. and U.S.S.R.

SAM — Surface-to-air missile. Used against aircraft and cruise missiles.

Satwar — Satellite warfare.

Seafarer — An extremely low frequency (ELF) transmitting system for communicating with submarines which the U.S. Navy tried to install in the United States.

Seaguard — An anti-submarine warfare research project being conducted by the Defense Advanced Research Projects Agency (DARPA).

Seasat — A new ocean dynamics satellite being designed in the U.S. Forerunner of a constellation of six satellites to monitor sea state conditions and other phenomena.

SES — Surface effect ship.

SHF — Super high frequency.

SIG — Stellar Inertial Guidance, a guidance system developed by the U.S. and probably also by the U.S.S.R.

SIRE — Satellite infrared experiment.

Skylab — A U.S. space laboratory.

SLBM — Submarine-launched ballistic missile.

SLCM — Sea-launched cruise missile.

Sonar — An acoustic device for sending and detecting underwater sound signals. Acronym for sound navigation and ranging.

SOSUS — Sound Surveillance System. The United States' ocean-wide underwater area surveillance system.

Spacetrack — The Air Force space surveillance system which is the backbone of SPADATS.

SPADATS — Space Detection and Tracking System.

Spartan — A U.S. anti-ballistic missile interceptor of 400 miles range.

Sprint — A U.S. anti-ballistic missile interceptor of 25 miles range.

Sputnik — The first series of U.S.S.R. satellites. The first satellite put in orbit.

SRAM — Short-range attack missile. Carried by bombers.

SRB — Special reentry body; an early maneuvering concept.

SS-9 — A large throw weight Soviet ICBM. Now being replaced with the SS-18.

SS-11 — A Soviet intercontinental ballistic missile. Now being replaced with SS-17 and SS-19 ICBMs.

SS-13 — A Soviet intercontinental ballistic missile with solid fuel.

SS-17 — A new generation Soviet intercontinental ballistic missile.

SS-18 — A new generation large throw weight Soviet intercontinental ballistic missile.

SS-19 — A new generation Soviet intercontinental ballistic missile.

SSBN — A nuclear-powered ballistic-missile-launching submarine.

SS-N-4 — An old Soviet submarine-launched ballistic missile.

SS-N-5 — An old Soviet submarine-launched ballistic missile.

SS-N-6 — A Soviet submarine-launched ballistic missile.

SS-N-8 — A Soviet submarine-launched ballistic missile.

SS-N-17 — A new generation Soviet submarine-launched ballistic missile.

SS-N-18 — A new generation Soviet submarine-launched ballistic missile.

Strategic — Having to do with strategy; the planning and directing of large scale military operations, as distinguished from tactical. In the case of nuclear weapons this is global in scope.

Strategic triad — The combination of land-based intercontinental ballistic missiles, airborne intercontinental bombers and cruise missiles, and submarine-launched ballistic missiles making up the strategic forces of the U.S. and U.S.S.R.

SUBROC — Submarine rocket, fired from submarines to destroy enemy submarines.

Tacamo — An airborne very low frequency broadcasting system to communicate with U.S. submarines.

Tactical — Having to do with tactics; arranging and maneuvering military forces in action or before the enemy. Usually associated with theatre operations such as Europe or Korea.

Teal Ruby — A mosaic infrared sensor being developed by the U.S. to detect bombers and cruise missiles. It will be satellite borne.

TERCOM — Terrain contour matching, a sensor system being developed to guide cruise missiles and home maneuvering warheads to their target.

Thor — A U.S. rocket booster motor.

Throw weight — The weight of a missile remaining after the last booster rocket has separated. Also called payload.

Time urgent targets — Military targets that would have to be destroyed quickly before they can launch weapons against the U.S.

Titan-2 — The United States' oldest intercontinental ballistic missile still in service. Also the largest.

Tomahawk — Name of the Navy's sea-launched cruise missile (SLCM).

Tracker — An older carrier-based anti-submarine warfare airplane. Also designated the S-2. Being replaced by S-3A Vikings.

Trajectory — The ballistic arc through which a ballistic missile travels.

UHF — Ultra high frequency.

Viking — The United States' new carrier-based anti-submarine warfare airplane. Also designated the S-3A.

VLF — Very low frequency.

VPX — Designation of the next generation U.S. long-range land-based anti-submarine warfare aircraft.

V/STOL — Vertical/short take-off and landing aircraft.

Warhead — The nuclear bomb of a strategic weapon. In the case of ballistic missiles the reentry vehicle which encases the nuclear bomb is often referred to as the warhead.

Yankee class submarine — A Soviet nuclear-powered ballistic missile submarine.

Yield — The explosive force of a nuclear bomb measured in kilotons or megatons.

IPS PUBLICATIONS

Dubious Specter:
A Skeptical Look
at the 'Soviet Threat'
By Fred Kaplan

A thorough exposition and analysis of the myths and realities surrounding the current U.S.-Soviet "military balance." Kaplan's comparisons of U.S. and Soviet nuclear arsenals and strategies provide the necessary background for understanding current debates on arms limitations and rising military costs. $4.95.

The Rise and Fall
of the 'Soviet Threat':
Domestic Sources of the
Cold War Consensus
By Alan Wolfe

A timely essay which demonstrates that American fear of the Soviet Union tends to fluctuate due to domestic factors, not in relation to the military and foreign policies of the USSR. Wolfe contends that recurring features of American domestic politics periodically coalesce to spur anti-Soviet sentiment, contributing to increased tensions and dangerous confrontations. $4.95.

Resurgent Militarism
By Michael T. Klare
and the Bay Area Chapter
of the Inter-University Committee

An analysis of the origins and consequences of the growing militaristic fervor which is spreading from Washington across the nation. The study examines America's changing strategic position since Vietnam and the political and economic forces which underlie the new upsurge in militarism. $2.00.

The Counterforce Syndrome:
A Guide to U.S. Nuclear Weapons
and Strategic Doctrine
By Robert C. Aldridge

An identification of how "counterforce" has replaced "deterrence" as the Pentagon's prevailing doctrine, contrary to what most Americans believe. This thorough summary and analysis of U.S. strategic nuclear weapons and military doctrine includes descriptions of MIRVs, MARVs, Trident systems, cruise missiles, and M-X missiles as they relate to the aims of a U.S. first strike. $4.95.

The Giants
Russia and America
By Richard Barnet

An authoritative, comprehensive account of the latest stage of the complex U.S.-Soviet relationship; how it came about, what has changed, and where it is headed.

"A thoughtful and balanced account of American-Soviet relations. Barnet goes beyond current controversies to discuss the underlying challenges of a relationship that is crucial to world order." —Cyril E. Black, Director, Center for International Studies, Princeton University

"An extraordinarily useful contribution to the enlightenment of the people of this country. . . . It is of fundamental importance that we understand the true state of our relations with Russia if we are to avoid a tragic mistake in our future."—Senator J.W. Fulbright. $4.95.

The New Generation
of Nuclear Weapons
By Stephen Daggett

An updated summary of strategic weapons, including American and Soviet nuclear hardware. These precarious new technologies may provoke startling shifts in strategic policy, leading planners to consider fighting "limited nuclear wars" or consider a preemptive first strike capability. $2.00.

Toward World Security:
A Program for Disarmament
By Earl C. Ravenal

This proposal argues that in light of destabilizing new strategic weapons systems and increasing regional conflicts which could involve the superpowers, the U.S. should take independent steps toward disarmament by not deploying new "counterforce" weapons, pledging no first use of nuclear weapons, and by following a non-interventionist foreign policy. $2.00.

Peace In Search of Makers
Riverside Church Reverse the Arms Race Convocation
Jane Rockman, Editor

A compilation of papers denouncing the proliferation of sophisticated weaponry, which threatens a nuclear cataclysm and destroys our society by diverting resources from social services and programs. This volume confronts the moral, economic, strategic and ethical aspects of the arms race and appeals for a citizen coalition to reverse the course of social decay and uncontrolled nuclear armament. Contributions by Richard Barnet, Michael Klare, Cynthia Arnson, Marcus Raskin and others. $5.95.

Assassination on Embassy Row
By John Dinges and Saul Landau

A devastating political document that probes all aspects of the Letelier-Moffitt assassinations, interweaving the investigations of the murder by the FBI and the Institute. The story surpasses the most sophisticated fiction in depth of characterization at the same time that it raises serious and tantalizing questions about the response of American intelligence and foreign policy to international terrorism. $14.95.

Supplying Repression:
U.S. Support for Authoritarian Regimes Abroad
By Michael T. Klare

A description of how the U.S. continues to supply arms and training to police and other internal security forces of repressive governments abroad. "Very important, fully documented indictment of U.S. role in supplying rightist Third World governments with the weaponry and know-how of repression." —*The Nation*. $4.95.

After the Shah
By Fred Halliday

Important background information on the National Front, the Tudeh Party, the religious opposition and many other groups whose policies and programs will determine Iran's future. $2.00.

A Continent Beseiged:
Foreign Military Activities
in Africa Since 1975
By Daniel Volman

A study of the growing military involvement of the two superpowers and their allies in Africa. Challenging the usual exclusive focus on Soviet and Cuban activities, the study suggests that the continuing escalation of French and American involvement threatens to engulf the continent in armed chaos and to bring the two superpowers into direct confrontation. Contains extensive data on African arms trade, the strength of African military forces, and the role of foreign military personnel. $2.00.

The Lean Years
Politics in the Age of Scarcity
By Richard J. Barnet

A lucid and startling analysis of basic global resources: energy, non-fuel minerals, food, water, and human labor. The depletion and maldistribution of supplies bodes a new global economic, political and military order in the 1980s.

" . . . brilliantly informed book . . . cogent, aphoristic pulling together of the skeins of catastrophic scarcity in 'the coming postpetroleum world' . . . "—*Publishers Weekly.* $12.95.

Feeding the Few:
Corporate Control of Food
By Susan George

The author of *How the Other Half Dies* has extended her critique of the world food system which is geared toward profit not people. This study draws the links between the hungry at home and those abroad exposing the economic and political forces pushing us towards a unified global food system. $4.95.

How the Other Half Dies
By Susan George

This important examination of multinational agribusiness corporations explains that the roots of hunger are not over-population, changing climate, or bad weather, but rather the control of food by the rich.

"A most intelligent, urgent and thought-provoking book on a truly vital subject."—*John Kenneth Galbraith.* $5.95.

Human Rights, Economic Aid and Private Banks: The Case of Chile
By Michael Moffitt and Isabel Letelier

This issue paper documents the tremendous increase in private bank loans to the Chilean military dictatorship since the overthrow of Salvador Allende in 1973. Previously unpublished data demonstrates how private banks rescued the Chilean military government by increasing loans to Chile at the very time governments and international institutions were reducing their loans because of massive human rights violations. $2.00.

Decoding Corporate Camouflage: U.S. Business Support for Apartheid
By Elizabeth Schmidt

By exposing the decisive role of U.S. corporations in sustaining apartheid, this study places highly-touted employment "reforms" in the context of the systematic economic exploitation and political repression of the black South African majority. Schmidt charges that the Sullivan Principles—the fair employment code devised by American corporations to deflect public criticism of their South African activities—are scanty cover for U.S. capital, technology, and know-how that support the white minority regime.

" . . .forcefully presented."—Kirkus Reviews. $4.95.

South Africa: Foreign Investment and Apartheid
By Lawrence Litvak, Robert DeGrasse, Kathleen McTigue

A critical examination of the argument that multinationals and foreign investment are a force for progressive change in South Africa. This study carefully documents the role that foreign investment has played in sustaining apartheid. $3.95.

Black South Africa Explodes
By Counter Information Services

The only detailed account available of events in South Africa in the first year since the uprising which began in June 1976 in Soweto. The report exposes the reality of life in the African townships, the impact of South Africa's economic crisis on blacks, and the white regime's dependence on European and American finance. $2.95.